# SALAD AND SOUP BOOK

# Annie Lerman's New

# SALAD SOUP AND BOOK

Running Press
Book Publishers
Philadelphia, Pennsylvania

International representative: Kaiman & Polon, Inc.
2175 Lemoine Avenue, Fort Lee, New Jersey 07024.


9   8   7   6   5   4   3   2   1
Digit on the right indicates the number of this printing.

*Library of Congress Cataloging in Publication Data:*

*Lerman, Ann, 1942-*
  *Soup and salad book.*

*Summary: Recipes for more than 250 soups and salads
and 40 salad dressings.*
*1. Soups.  2. Salads.  [1. Soups.  2. Salads.*
*3. Cookery]  I. Title.*
*TX757.L44  1983    641.8'13    83-9178*

ISBN:  0-89471-235-7 (paperback)
ISBN:  0-89471-236-5 (library binding)

Newly edited by Laura Fortenbaugh.
Drawings by Teresa Anderko.

Cover design by Toby Schmidt.

Typography: *Text:* Souvenir, by CompArt, Philadelphia.
*Headings:* Roman Script.
Printed by Port City Press, Baltimore, Maryland.


This book may be ordered by mail from the publisher. Please include 75 cents
postage. **But try your bookstore first.**


Running Press
Book Publishers
125 South 22nd Street
Philadelphia, Pennsylvania 19103

# Contents

# Soups

# First Words
# on Soups

Soups have an ancient and humble origin. Throughout recorded history, a loaf of bread and a bowl of soup have been nutritious staples. Whether homey or elegant, a soup can include practically any ingredients and be enjoyed at any time of day.

A flavorful soup starts with a stock that's rich in food value. When you're cooking vegetables, be sure to reserve all the liquid, as well as the water used for sprouting; the juices from drained, stewed, or soaked dried fruit; fish juices; and meat and poultry juices from which the fat has been skimmed or otherwise removed. Refrigerate these nutritious liquids in screw-top jars and use them in recipes in place of plain water. Adding raw vegetable scraps will also enhance any stock's flavor and food value.

Before beginning any of these recipes, assemble all the ingredients you'll need. (For each soup, the appropriate stock is printed in bold face for quick reference.) It's also wise to use the items suggested in the list under "Basic Kitchen Equipment" (see page 176) and in the recipes themselves.

You can prepare stocks well in advance and either store them in the refrigerator or freeze them. Don't remove the fat that rises to the surface until the stock is ready to be used: this layer seals out air and helps preserve the liquid underneath. When home-made stock is not available, then dehydrated chicken, beef, or vegetable broth (in cube or granular form) is a convenient alternative. But when preparing recipes with dehydrated broth—which tends to be salty—be careful of the amount of extra salt you add.

There are also several very good canned chicken and beef broths available. Try different brands to see which you like best. Stocks that are not available commercially—those that you can't substitute for and which you have to make from the recipes in the first section of this book—head the list of ingredients in the recipes that follow.

With a quantity of stock on hand, most of the soups in this book can be prepared fairly quickly. Adding a variety of ingredients to your basic stocks will result in a soup that requires a minimum of extra cooking time: in fact, these soups should be

Soups

simmered only long enough for their ingredients to become tender. Fruits and vegetables that are cubed, diced, or shredded need to be cooked in the stock for only a very brief time, so as to retain their nutritional values, color, and texture. Freshly-made soups cooked this way should be served immediately after preparation.

With the help of a blender or food processor, you can whip up a delicious home-made soup in just a few minutes. Simply combine fresh or frozen vegetables with a liquid—such as yogurt, broth, or juice—and blend until perfectly smooth. In minutes, this transforms uncooked puréed vegetables into a fresh garden soup without losing any of the essential vitamins. These delicious instant-energy soups store well in covered containers in the refrigerator. Shake well before serving, and pour out a quick, healthful drink.

Soups prepared with dried ingredients need a longer, slower cooking time. To speed the process up a bit, soak dried fruits or vegetables before using them. Simmer these soups until the ingredients are quite tender; this will also give the flavors time to blend.

Even if you've never cooked a soup before, it won't be long until you'll be tempted to add your own personal touches to your favorite recipes. An herb, vegetable, or starch will add flavor or create a new texture. Yogurt, sour cream, buttermilk, and cream can all be interchanged or combined for variations of taste. But don't let your imagination stop with the preparations.

Traditionally, soups mark the beginning of a meal. Served with a crusty loaf of bread, a hearty hot soup makes a meal in itself. To give balance to a variety of dishes, a cup of bouillon can be enjoyed throughout the meal. A light and refreshing chilled fruit soup is a delightful palate-cleanser between courses. In the hot summer, a chilled soup also makes a refreshing pick-me-up; while on a cold wintry day, hot soup together with a grilled sandwich can make a very wholesome lunch. Serve soups at any time and present them in different ways to suit the season and the occasion. And for a light conclusion to any meal, try a fruit soup with a board of assorted cheeses.

Clear glass or white bowls best complement a chilled soup. Rest a glass bowl on a bed of crushed ice, or serve your soup more informally in a frosty mug. Hot soups are best in a warm tureen or warm earthenware bowl. A variety of garnishes will add nourishment as well as eye appeal. Snipped herbs, grated or chopped raw vegetables, nuts, seeds, blossoms, or thinly-sliced fruits and vegetables will enhance the soup bowl or tureen.

—Annie Lerman

# Stocks

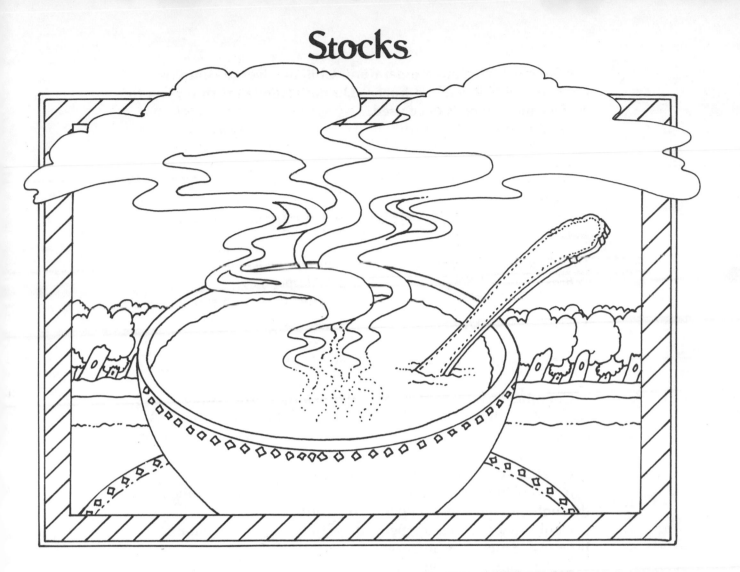

## Chicken Stock

3 quarts water
4 pounds chicken, disjointed,
   and giblets, omit liver
1 large onion
2 carrots
2 stalks celery, halved

1 tablespoon salt
bouquet garni of 6 sprigs
   parsley, 2 sprigs thyme, 1
    bay leaf, and 4 peppercorns
salt to taste

Bring water to boil in large kettle. Add chicken and giblets. Skim off froth as it rises to surface. Lower heat to simmer. Add onion, carrots, celery, salt, and bouquet garni. If necessary add boiling water to keep ingredients barely covered. Cover and simmer mixture for about 1 1/2 hours.

Remove chicken from kettle. Remove meat from carcass, reserving for later use. Return carcass to kettle and continue to simmer for about 1 hour. Add salt to taste.

Remove and discard carcass and bouquet garni. Strain stock through fine sieve, pressing hard on solids.

Soups

13

Cool stock at room temperature. Chill in covered container for later use. Stock may be frozen. Do not remove fat that rises to surface until stock is to be used.

Makes about 2 1/2 quarts.

# Turkey Stock

1 roasted turkey carcass,
  broken up
3 quarts water
1 onion
1 carrot
1 leek

1 turnip, chopped
1 tablespoon salt
bouquet garni of 6 sprigs
  parsley, 2 sprigs thyme, 1
  bay leaf, and 4 peppercorns
salt to taste

Combine turkey carcass and water in large kettle. Bring to boil. Skim off froth as it rises to surface. Lower heat to simmer. Add onion, carrot, leek, turnip, salt, and bouquet garni. If necessary add boiling water to keep ingredients barely covered. Cover and simmer mixture for about 2 1/2 hours. Add salt to taste.

Remove and discard carcass and bouquet garni. Strain stock through fine sieve, pressing hard on solids.

Cool stock at room temperature. Chill in covered container for later use. Stock may be frozen.

Makes about 2 1/2 quarts.

# Giblet Stock

giblets from 1 fowl (omit liver)
1 cup water
1 cup chicken stock
1 small onion

1 small carrot
bouquet garni of 3 sprigs parsley,
  1 sprig thyme, 1/2 bay leaf
salt to taste

Combine giblets, water, and chicken stock in saucepan. Bring to boil. Skim off froth as it rises to surface. Lower heat to simmer. Add onion, carrot, and bouquet garni. Cover and simmer mixture for about 1 hour. Add salt to taste.

Remove and discard bouquet garni. Strain stock through fine sieve, pressing hard on solids. Cool stock at room temperature. Chill in covered container for later use. Stock may be frozen.

Makes about 1 1/2 cups.

Soups

# Consommé

3 quarts water
3 pounds chicken, disjointed
1 pound lean beef
1 pound veal bones
1 pound marrow bones
2 teaspoons salt
1/4 teaspoon celery salt
1/4 teaspoon nutmeg

bouquet garni of 4 peppercorns,
   2 sprigs thyme, and 6 sprigs
   parsley
1 onion
2 carrots, trimmed
2 stalks celery and tops, halved
salt to taste

Combine water and chicken in large kettle. Bring to boil. Skim off froth as it rises to surface. Lower heat to simmer. Add beef, veal bones, marrow bones, salt, celery salt, nutmeg, bouquet garni, onion, carrots, and celery. If necessary add boiling water to keep ingredients barely covered. Cover and simmer for about 4 hours. Add salt to taste.

Remove chicken and beef. Remove and discard bones and bouquet garni. Strain consommé through sieve lined with double thickness of cheesecloth. Press hard on solids.

Cool consommé at room temperature. Chill in covered container for later use. Do not remove fat that rises to surface until consommé is to be used. Consommé may be frozen.

Makes about 2 1/2 quarts.

# Bouillon

3 1/2 quarts water
2 pounds chicken, disjointed
2 pounds lean brisket
2 pounds shin bones
2 teaspoons salt
1/8 teaspoon cayenne

bouquet garni of 1 bay leaf, 6
   sprigs parsley, 2 peppercorns, and 2 sprigs thyme
1 onion
2 carrots, trimmed
1 stalk celery and top, halved
salt to taste

Combine water, chicken, brisket, and bones in large kettle. Bring to boil. Skim off froth as it rises to surface. Lower heat to simmer. Add salt, cayenne, bouquet garni, onion, carrots, and

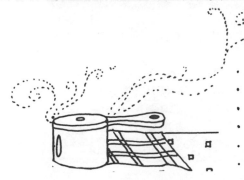

## ANNIE'S TIPS

Place ingredients for bouquet garni in the center of a square piece of cheesecloth. Fold cheesecloth in half. Sew edges together with white thread. Leave a six-inch-long thread to hang over edge of pot. Bouquet garni may be prepared in a tea ball if fresh herbs and seeds are used.

celery. If necessary add boiling water to keep ingredients barely covered. Cover and simmer for about 1 1/2 hours.

Remove brisket and chicken parts from kettle. Remove meat from chicken bones. Reserve brisket and chicken for later use.

Return chicken bones to kettle. Cover and simmer for about 1 hour. Add salt to taste.

Remove and discard shin bones, chicken bones, and bouquet garni. Strain bouillon through fine sieve, pressing hard on solids.

Cool bouillon at room temperature. Chill in covered container for later use. Do not remove fat that rises to surface until bouillon is to be used. Bouillon may be frozen.

Makes about 3 quarts.

# Beef Stock

*3 pounds beef, with bones*
*3 quarts water*
*1 onion*
*1 carrot*
*1 stalk celery, halved*
*1 tomato, quartered*

*1 tablespoon salt*
*bouquet garni of 6 sprigs*
*parsley, 4 peppercorns, and 2*
*sprigs thyme*
*salt to taste*

Combine beef with bones and water in kettle. Bring to boil. Skim off froth as it rises to surface. Lower heat to simmer. Add onion, carrot, celery, tomato, salt, and bouquet garni. If necessary add boiling water to keep ingredients barely covered. Cover and simmer mixture for about 1 1/2 hours. Add salt to taste.

Remove beef with bones and reserve beef for later use. Remove and discard bouquet garni. Strain stock through fine sieve, pressing hard on solids.

Cool stock at room temperature. Chill in covered container for later use. Do not remove fat that rises to surface until stock is to be used. Stock may be frozen.

Makes about 2 1/2 quarts.

ANNIE'S TIPS

Draw a spoon across the surface of the hot liquid to skim froth.

# Lamb Stock

2 pounds lamb shanks, cracked
7 cups water
1 onion
1 carrot
1 stalk celery, halved

1 teaspoon salt
bouquet garni of 1 bay leaf, 3
    sprigs parsley, and 2 pepper-
    corns
salt to taste

Combine lamb shanks and water in kettle. Bring to boil. Skim off froth as it rises to surface. Lower heat to simmer. Add onion, carrot, celery, salt, and bouquet garni. If necessary add boiling water to keep ingredients barely covered. Cover and simmer mixture for about 2 hours. Add salt to taste.

Remove lamb shanks, reserving lamb for later use. Remove and discard bouquet garni. Strain stock through fine sieve, pressing hard on solids.

Cool stock at room temperature. Chill in covered container for later use. Do not remove fat that rises to surface until stock is to be used. Stock may be frozen.

Makes about 1 1/2 quarts.

# Basic Fish Stock

1–1 1/2 pounds whole fish, cut
    into large pieces (such as
    flounder, haddock, sole,
    whiting, or tile)
2 stalks celery and tops, sliced
1 onion, sliced
1 carrot, sliced
1/2 teaspoon salt

bouquet garni of 1 bay leaf, 1/4
    teaspoon fennel seeds, 1/4
    teaspoon dill seeds, 2 table-
    spoons dried parsley leaves,
    and 1/4 teaspoon dulse (op-
    tional)
4 cups water
salt and pepper to taste

Combine fish, celery, onion, carrot, salt, and bouquet garni in heavy saucepan. Add water. If necessary add more water to cover ingredients. Bring to boil. Lower heat. Cover and simmer for about 30 minutes.

Remove and discard bouquet garni. Add salt and pepper to taste.

Strain stock through fine sieve, pressing hard on solids.

Cool stock at room temperature. Chill in covered container for later use. Stock may be frozen. Basic fish stock may be used at once.

Makes about 3 1/2 cups.

Soups

# Puréed Fish Stock

2 large onions, sliced
4 tablespoons salad oil
3 pounds assorted fish steaks
  (bass, whiting, porgy, sole,
  tile)
4 large tomatoes, cut into
  chunks

1 quart water
1 teaspoon salt
bouquet garni of 6 sprigs
  thyme, 6 sprigs parsley, 1
  bay leaf, and 4 peppercorns
salt to taste

Combine onions and salad oil in kettle. Sauté for about 2 minutes or until onions are crisp tender. Stir in fish steaks and tomatoes. Continue stirring and simmer for about 10 minutes. Stir in water, salt, and bouquet garni. Bring mixture to boil. Lower heat and simmer in covered kettle for about 20 minutes.

Remove and discard bouquet garni and any heavy bones that may be in stock.

In batches, transfer fish mixture to blender or food processor. Blend until smooth.

Return purée to kettle. Simmer for 5 minutes. Add salt to taste.

Cool puréed stock at room temperature. Chill in covered container for later use. Stock may be frozen. Puréed fish stock may be used at once.

**Makes about 3 quarts.**

Soups

# White Fish Stock

2 tablespoons salad oil
1 onion, sliced
1 pound fish, bones, and skin
   from any white fish (such as
   flounder, sole, or whiting)
4 cups water
1 carrot

1/2 teaspoon salt
bouquet garni of 12 sprigs
   parsley and 1/2 bay leaf
3 tablespoons lemon juice
1/2 cup dry white wine
salt and pepper to taste

Combine salad oil and onion in heavy saucepan. Sauté for about 2 minutes or until onions are crisp tender. Stir in fish, bones, fish skin, and water. Bring mixture to boil. Skim off froth as it rises to surface. Lower heat to simmer. Add carrot, salt, bouquet garni, lemon juice, and wine. If necessary add boiling water to keep ingredients barely covered. Cover and simmer for about 25 minutes. Add salt and pepper to taste.

Remove and discard bouquet garni. Strain stock through fine sieve, pressing hard on solids.

Cool stock at room temperature. Chill in covered container for later use. White fish stock may be used at once.

Makes about 4 cups.

# Vegetable Stock

6 cups water
4 carrots, sliced
1 onion
2 stalks celery, halved
2 leeks, cut into chunks
1/2 pound green beans, snapped

2 zucchini, sliced
2 tomatoes, cut into chunks
1/2 pound mushroom stems
4 sprigs parsley
1 1/2 tablespoons soy sauce

Combine all ingredients except soy sauce in kettle. Bring to boil. Lower heat to simmer. Cover and simmer for about 1 hour. Add soy sauce. Cover and simmer for about 10 minutes.

Strain stock through sieve lined with double thickness of cheesecloth. Squeeze cheesecloth to extract all stock.

Vegetable stock may be used at once. Cool stock at room temperature; chill or freeze in covered container for later use.

Makes about 7 cups.

## ANNIE'S TIPS

Reserve water from steamed vegetables to be used as vegetable water.

Soups

19

# Green Vegetable Stock

6 cups water
1/4 cup dried mushrooms,
  rinsed
1/2 cup split peas, green or
  yellow
1/2 pound fresh mushrooms,
  soaked and wiped
1 large potato, cut into chunks
1 onion
2 carrots, cut into chunks

2 stalks celery, with tops, cut
  into chunks
1 cup green beans, snapped
2 zucchini, cut into chunks
4 sprigs parsley
1 1/2 teaspoons salt
1/4 cup nutritional yeast (optional)
salt and pepper to taste

Combine water, dried mushrooms, and split peas in large saucepan. Bring to boil. Lower heat. Cover and simmer for about 1 hour.

Add mushrooms, potato, onion, carrots, celery, green beans, zucchini, and parsley. Bring to boil. Lower heat. Cover and simmer for about 30 minutes.

Strain stock through sieve lined with double thickness of cheesecloth. Squeeze cheesecloth to extract all of stock. Return stock to saucepan. Stir in salt and nutritional yeast. Add salt and pepper to taste.

Green Vegetable Stock may be used at once. Cool stock at room temperature. Chill in covered container for later use. Stock may also be frozen.

Makes about 5 cups.


# Coconut Milk

(not coconut water)

3 cups water
2 cups unsweetened coconut,
  grated

Put water in saucepan. Stir in coconut. Bring mixture to boil.

Remove saucepan from heat. Cover and allow to stand for 30 minutes.

Strain coconut mixture through sieve lined with double thickness of cheesecloth. Squeeze cheesecloth to extract all coconut milk.

Cool coconut milk at room temperature. Chill coconut milk in covered container for later use. Coconut milk may be used at once. (Before using prepared chilled coconut milk, heat to blend.)

Makes about 2 1/2 cups.

# Centerpiece Soups

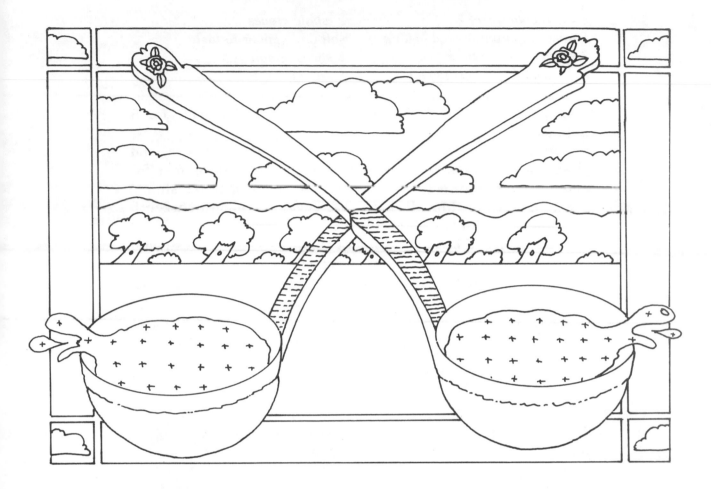

# Split Pea Soup

**2 cups beef stock**
*6 cups water*
*2 cups dried split peas*

*bouquet garni of 1 bay leaf and
    1 teaspoon thyme*
*3 carrots, chopped fine*
*2 tablespoons dried parsley*

In large saucepan combine beef stock, water, dried split peas, and bouquet garni. Bring mixture to boil. Lower heat, cover, and simmer for 1 1/2 hours. Add carrots. Simmer uncovered for 20 minutes. Stir occasionally.

Remove and discard bouquet garni. Stir in parsley.

**Serve soup in warm tureen or warm individual soup bowls.
Makes 6 servings.**

Soups

# Jelled Cranberry Bouillon Cup

1/4 cup cold water
1 tablespoon unflavored gelatin
**2 cups turkey stock**
1 cup jellied cranberry sauce

2 whole cloves
salt and pepper to taste
5 slices lemon
bread sticks

Combine water and gelatin in small bowl. Set aside for 5 minutes.

Combine turkey stock, cranberry sauce, gelatin mixture, and cloves in saucepan. Bring to boil. Lower heat and simmer for about 5 minutes, or until smooth. Add salt and pepper to taste.

Strain mixture through fine sieve. Divide bouillon between 5 bouillon cups. Chill for about 4 hours.

Break up jelled bouillon with fork before serving. Garnish with lemon slice on edge of each cup. Serve with bread sticks.

**Makes 5 servings.**

# Cream of Tomato Soup

3 tablespoons margarine
1 onion, chopped
3 cups tomatoes, canned or
  fresh, chopped
1/2 teaspoon salt
1 teaspoon sugar
2 tablespoons flour

1/4 teaspoon baking soda
**1 cup chicken stock**
1 cup sour cream
salt and pepper to taste
snipped dill or fresh minced
  basil

Combine margarine and onion in saucepan. Sauté onion for about 3 minutes, or until tender.

Transfer onion to blender or food processor. Add tomatoes, salt, sugar, flour, and baking soda. Blend until smooth.

Transfer tomato mixture to saucepan. Stir in chicken stock and sour cream. Stir and heat soup to simmer. Do not boil. Add salt and pepper to taste.

Serve soup in warm tureen or warm individual soup bowls. Garnish with snipped dill or minced basil.

**Makes 4 servings.**

**Soups**

ANNIE'S TIPS

Cold soup requires more seasoning than hot soup. Taste-test the soup after chilling.

# Chilled Cucumber Soup

**1 cup chicken stock**
1/2 cup currants or raisins
1/3 cup ground walnuts
1 cup yogurt
1 cup light cream or half-and-half
1 hard-boiled egg, minced

1/4 cup scallions, white part only, chopped fine
1 cucumber, peeled and chopped
salt and pepper to taste
snipped dill

Combine chicken stock and currants in saucepan. Bring to boil. Remove from heat. Set aside.

Combine walnuts, yogurt, light cream, egg, scallions, and cucumber in mixing bowl. Whisk in currant mixture.

Chill in covered container for about 4 hours. Add salt and pepper to taste.

Serve in glass bowls. Garnish with snipped dill.

Makes 4 servings.

Soups

# Barley and Vegetable Soup

**4 cups chicken stock**
1/3 cup barley
3 tablespoons margarine
2 stalks celery, chopped
2 carrots, chopped
1 leek, chopped

1 tablespoon margarine
1/2 pound mushrooms, soaked,
   wiped, and chopped
salt and pepper to taste
1/2 cup chopped parsley

Heat chicken stock in saucepan. Bring stock to boil. Add barley. Lower heat. Cover and simmer for about 20 minutes.

In skillet sauté celery, carrots, and leek in 3 tablespoons margarine for 2 minutes. Add mixture to saucepan. Sauté mushrooms in 1 tablespoon margarine for 1 minute. Add mushrooms to saucepan.

Simmer soup for 15 minutes, or until barley and vegetables are tender. Add salt and pepper to taste.

Serve soup in warm tureen or warm individual soup bowls. Garnish with chopped parsley.

Makes 4 servings.

# Buckwheat and Potato Soup

**4 cups chicken stock**
2 large potatoes, peeled and
   diced
1 large onion, chopped
1/4 cup medium buckwheat
   groats

salt and pepper to taste
1 cup evaporated milk
1 teaspoon dried parsley flakes
1 teaspoon dried thyme

Combine chicken stock, potatoes, onion, and buckwheat groats in covered saucepan. Bring mixture to boil. Lower heat and simmer for about 12 minutes, or until potatoes are tender. Add salt and pepper to taste. Stir in evaporated milk, parsley, and thyme. Simmer soup for 5 minutes. Do not boil.

Serve soup in warm tureen or warm individual soup bowls.

Makes 4 servings.

ANNIE'S TIPS

If a jell_ _ _ lène is desired, combine 1 tablespoon unflavored gelatin and ½ cup water. Add softened gelatin to soup before chilling.

# Asparagus Potato Chowder

2 cups chicken stock
3 medium red-skinned potatoes, peeled and diced
1 small onion, chopped
1/2 teaspoon salt
1/8 teaspoon ground nutmeg

10 ounce package frozen cut asparagus
salt and pepper to taste
1 1/2 cups half-and-half or light cream
4-ounce package cream cheese with pimiento, softened

Combine chicken stock, potatoes, onion, salt, and nutmeg in saucepan. Bring mixture to boil. Lower heat. Cover and simmer for about 5 minutes. Add frozen asparagus and return mixture to boil. Lower heat. Cover and simmer for about 5 minutes, or until vegetables are crisp tender. Add salt and pepper to taste.

In mixing bowl blend softened cream cheese with half-and-half or light cream. Stir mixture into saucepan. Continue stirring until blended. Do not boil.

Serve at once in warm tureen or warm individual soup bowls.
Makes 4 servings.

# Chilled Garden Madrilène

2 1/2 cups crushed tomatoes
2 1/2 cups consommé
2 tablespoons dry sherry
1 stalk celery, minced
1 small onion, minced
1 small carrot, minced
1/2 medium cucumber, minced

1/2 medium green pepper, minced
1/2 teaspoon salt
1 sprig parsley, minced
1/4 teaspoon thyme, crushed
salt and pepper to taste
sour cream

Combine all ingredients except sour cream in mixing bowl. Chill in covered container for about 4 hours. Add salt and pepper to taste.

Serve in glass bowls. Garnish with dollops of sour cream.
Makes 6 servings.

Soups

# Chicken Fried Rice Soup

**4 cups chicken stock**
1/4 cup salad oil
1/4 cup scallions, sliced thin
1 stalk celery, chopped
2 cloves garlic, minced

1 large egg, beaten
1 cup cooked rice
1/4 cup bean sprouts
2 tablespoons soy sauce
crisp Oriental noodles

Heat chicken stock in saucepan to simmer.

Combine salad oil, scallions, celery, and garlic in skillet. Sauté mixture for about 3 minutes. Add egg and scramble. Add rice, bean sprouts, and soy sauce to egg mixture. Add rice mixture to chicken stock.

Serve soup in warm tureen or warm individual soup bowls. Garnish with crisp Oriental noodles.

Makes 4 servings.

# Turkey and Barley Soup

3 tablespoons salad oil
1 onion, minced
2 tablespoons salad oil
1 small carrot, diced
1 stalk celery, diced
1 cup mushrooms, soaked,
   wiped, and chopped

**6 1/2 cups turkey stock**
1/4 cup pearl barley
3/4 teaspoon marjoram
1/4 teaspoon salt
salt and pepper to taste

Combine 3 tablespoons salad oil and onion in large saucepan. Sauté onion for about 2 minutes. Add 2 tablespoons salad oil, carrot, celery, and mushrooms. Sauté for about 5 minutes. Add turkey stock, barley, marjoram, and salt. Bring mixture to boil. Lower heat. Cover and simmer, stirring occasionally, for about 1 hour and 15 minutes, or until barley is very tender. Add salt and pepper to taste.

Serve soup in warm tureen or warm individual soup bowls.
**Makes 6 servings.**

# Apricot Lentil Soup

**6 cups lamb stock or beef stock**
*1 onion, diced*
*1 cup lentils, rinsed*
*1/2 teaspoon salt*
*2 medium potatoes, peeled and
   diced*

*1 cup dried apricots, diced*
*1/3 cup chopped walnuts*
*1/2 teaspoon tarragon*
*salt and pepper to taste*

Combine lamb stock, onion, lentils, and salt in large saucepan. Bring to boil. Lower heat. Cover and simmer for about 1 hour. Add potatoes, apricots, walnuts, and tarragon. Cover and simmer for about 20 minutes, or until potatoes are tender. Add salt and pepper to taste.

**Serve soup in warm tureen or warm individual soup bowls.**
**Makes 6 servings.**

Soups

# Sweet-Sour Cabbage Borscht

2 tablespoons salad oil
1 onion, diced
**8 cups beef stock**
1 pound can tomatoes, crushed
1/4 cup raisins
1 large head cabbage, shredded

1/2 teaspoon salt
1/4 teaspoon ground ginger
1/4 cup lemon juice
1/4 cup honey
honey or lemon juice to taste
salt and pepper to taste

Combine salad oil and onion in large saucepan. Sauté onion for about 2 minutes. Add beef stock, tomatoes, raisins, cabbage, and salt. Bring to boil. Lower heat. Cover and simmer for about 10 minutes. Stir in ginger, lemon juice, and honey. Continue to simmer for about 10 minutes. Add either honey or lemon juice, and salt and pepper to taste.

Serve soup in warm tureen or warm individual soup bowls.

Makes 8 servings.

# Tomato Celery Essence

**4 cups chicken stock**
1/2 bunch celery, washed,
   trimmed, and diced
1 cup canned tomatoes, drained
   and chopped

1 slice onion, diced
1/4 teaspoon thyme
1/2 teaspoon salt
salt and pepper to taste
4 sprigs parsley

Combine chicken stock and celery in saucepan. Bring mixture to boil. Lower heat. Cover and simmer for 30 minutes.

Combine tomatoes, onion, thyme, and salt in blender or food processor. Blend until smooth.

Strain celery broth. Discard celery. In saucepan, combine celery broth with tomato purée. Heat soup to boiling point. Add salt and pepper to taste.

Serve soup in warm tureen or warm individual soup bowls. Garnish with sprigs of parsley.

Makes 4 servings.

ANNIE'S TIPS

Chopped or shredded vegetables that will be added to soup only need to be cooked briefly. This method retains their food value.

# Chilled Carrot and Lettuce Bisque

**4 cups chicken stock**
5 medium carrots, shredded
2 tablespoons margarine
1 head Boston lettuce, shredded
1/4 cup scallions, minced

3 tablespoons margarine
1 cup sour cream
3/4 teaspoon chervil
4 egg yolks, beaten
salt and pepper to taste
sour cream

Heat chicken stock in saucepan to simmer. Remove from heat.

Combine carrots and 2 tablespoons margarine in saucepan. Sauté carrots for about 2 minutes. Transfer carrots to chicken stock.

Combine lettuce, scallions, and 3 tablespoons margarine in saucepan. Sauté for about 1 minute. Transfer vegetables to chicken stock. Stir in sour cream and chervil. Stir in beaten egg yolks.

Chill in covered container for about 4 hours. Add salt and pepper to taste.

Serve soup in glass bowls. Garnish with dollops of sour cream. Makes 6 servings.

Soups

# Chilled Squash and Carrot Bisque

*3 medium yellow summer
    squash, sliced*
*2 medium carrots, chopped*
*1/2 green pepper, seeded and
    chopped*
*1 small onion, sliced*
**1 cup chicken stock**

*1/2 teaspoon salt*
**1 cup chicken stock**
*13 1/2 ounce can evaporated
    milk*
*salt and pepper to taste*
*parsley sprigs*

Combine squash, carrots, green pepper, onion, 1 cup chicken stock, and salt in blender or food processor. Blend until smooth. Transfer mixture to mixing bowl. Stir in 1 cup chicken stock. Stir in evaporated milk.

Chill in covered container for about 4 hours. Add salt and pepper to taste.

Serve in glass bowls. Garnish with sprigs of parsley.

Makes 6 servings.

# Gazpacho

*4 tomatoes, quartered*
*1 cucumber, peeled and sliced*
*1 onion, sliced*
*1 green pepper, seeded and cut
    into chunks*
*1 clove garlic, crushed (op-
    tional)*
*2 tablespoons salad oil*
*2 tablespoons lemon juice*
*1/2 teaspoon salt*

*2–3 dashes cayenne*
*1/2 green pepper, chopped fine*
*1/2  cucumber, peeled and
    chopped fine*
*1/2 small onion, chopped fine*
*1 cup tomato juice*
**2 cups beef stock**
*salt to taste*
*cheese croutons*

Combine tomatoes, sliced cucumber, sliced onion, green pepper chunks, garlic, salad oil, lemon juice, salt, and cayenne in blender or food processor. Blend until smooth.

Transfer to mixing bowl. Stir in chopped green pepper, chopped cucumber, chopped onion, tomato juice, and beef stock.

Chill in covered container for about 4 hours. Add salt to taste.

Serve in glass bowls. Garnish with cheese croutons.

Makes 6 servings.

# Apricot Chicken Soup

4 ounces dried apricots,
  chopped
1 1/2 cups dry white wine
**3 cups chicken stock**
1/2 cup cooked chicken, diced

1 tablespoon chopped fresh
  basil
1/2 cup cooked rice, warm
salt and pepper to taste

Soak apricots in wine for 6 hours.

Combine chicken stock, chicken, and basil in saucepan. Add apricot and wine mixture. Bring to boil. Reduce heat and simmer for 25 minutes. Stir in rice. Add salt and pepper to taste.

Serve at once in warm tureen or warm individual soup bowls.

Makes 4 servings.

# Frosty Mint Soup

1/4 cup fine barley
**3 cups chicken stock**
1 slice onion, minced
1/3 cup finely chopped fresh
  mint

1 1/2 cups yogurt
1/4 teaspoon salt
salt and pepper to taste
8 sprigs mint

Combine barley, chicken stock, and onion in saucepan. Bring mixture to boil. Lower heat and simmer for about 30 minutes, or until barley is tender. Remove saucepan from heat. Stir in mint. Allow to cool at room temperature. Add yogurt and salt. Stir until soup is smooth.

Chill in covered container for about 6 hours. Add salt and pepper to taste.

Serve soup in glass bowls or chilled mugs. Garnish with sprigs of mint.

Makes 4 servings.

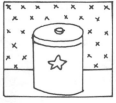

Soups

# Egg Drop Soup

**6 cups chicken stock**
10 ounce package chopped
  spinach
1/4 cup scallions, sliced very
  thin

3 eggs, beaten
3 cloves garlic, minced
1/4 teaspoon salt
salt and freshly ground white
  pepper to taste

Combine chicken stock, spinach, and scallions in saucepan. Bring mixture to boil. Lower heat. Cover and simmer for 5 minutes.

Combine eggs, garlic, and salt. Pour egg mixture into stock mixture in fine stream. Simmer soup for 2 minutes. Add salt and pepper to taste.

Serve at once in warm tureen or warm individual soup bowls.

**Makes 6 servings.**

Soups

## ANNIE'S TIPS

Reserve drained cooking water to use in other recipes as vegetable water.

# Ginger Okra Soup

1 cup cut okra, fresh or frozen
1 cup water
1/4 teaspoon salt
**4 cups chicken stock**

1 tablespoon peeled, shredded
   ginger root
salt and pepper to taste

Combine okra, water, and salt in saucepan. Bring to boil. Lower heat. Cover and simmer for about 5 minutes, or until okra is tender.

Drain okra in colander. Refresh under cold running water. Set aside.

Combine chicken stock and ginger root in saucepan. Bring to boil. Lower heat to simmer. Add okra. Add salt and pepper to taste.

Serve soup at once in warm individual soup bowls.

Makes 4 servings.

# Chilled Zucchini Soup

4 medium zucchini, sliced
1 medium onion, chopped
1/2 green pepper, chopped
**1 cup chicken stock**
1/2 teaspoon salt

2 cups yogurt or sour cream
salt and pepper to taste
1 tomato, peeled, seeded, and
   chopped
snipped chives

Combine zucchini, onion, green pepper, chicken stock, and salt in blender or food processor. Blend until smooth.

Transfer to mixing bowl. Whisk in yogurt. Chill in covered container for about 4 hours. Add salt and pepper to taste.

Serve in glass bowls. Garnish with chopped tomato and snipped chives.

Makes 6 servings.

# Minestrone

3 tablespoons salad oil
1 onion, chopped
1 clove garlic, minced
**8 cups beef stock**
2 medium carrots, diced
2 stalks celery and tops, sliced
1 cup string beans, snapped

1/4 cup minced parsley
1/8 teaspoon crushed red pepper (optional)
1/2 teaspoon thyme
1/2 teaspoon salt
4 ounces thin spaghetti, broken
1 pound can kidney beans

Soups

33

1 cup tomatoes, chopped
1 cup chopped cabbage

salt and pepper to taste
Parmesan cheese

Combine salad oil, onion, and garlic in large saucepan. Sauté for about 5 minutes.

Add beef stock, carrots, celery, string beans, tomatoes, cabbage, parsley, crushed red pepper, thyme, and salt. Bring to boil. Lower heat. Cover and simmer for about 15 minutes.

Bring soup to boil. Add spaghetti. Stir and cook for about 10 minutes. Stir in kidney beans. Add salt and pepper to taste.

Serve soup in warm tureen or warm individual soup bowls. Garnish with Parmesan cheese.

Makes 8 servings.

# Chilled Beet Borscht

2 tablespoons salad oil
1 onion, minced
2 pounds canned beets,
   drained, reserve juice
**2 cups beef stock**
1/4 teaspoon salt
1 tablespoon lemon juice

2 tablespoons honey
2 hard-boiled eggs, minced
1 cup sour cream
lemon juice or honey to taste
salt and pepper to taste
sour cream

Combine salad oil and onion in large saucepan. Sauté onion for about 3 minutes. Stir in reserved beet juice, beef stock, salt, lemon juice, and honey. Bring to boil. Lower heat. Cover and simmer for about 5 minutes.

Chop drained beets. Add beets to saucepan. Add either lemon juice or honey to taste.

Cool soup at room temperature. Whisk in minced egg and sour cream. Chill soup in covered container for about 4 hours. Add salt and pepper to taste.

Serve soup in glass bowls. Garnish with dollops of sour cream.

Makes 8 servings.

Soups

ANNIE'S TIPS

Store chilled soups in glass jars in the refrigerator. Shake and serve.

# Beef and Vegetable Soup

5 cups beef stock
2 carrots, diced
1 onion, chopped
2 stalks celery, diced
1 potato, peeled and diced
1 tomato, peeled, seeded, and
   chopped
1/2 cup peas

1/2 cup corn
1/4 teaspoon thyme
1/2 teaspoon salt
1/2 cup mushrooms, sliced
beef reserved from stock, cubed
2 tablespoons cornstarch
1/4 cup cold water
salt and pepper to taste

Combine beef stock with carrots, onion, celery, potato, tomato, peas, corn, thyme and salt in saucepan. Bring mixture to boil. Lower heat. Cover and simmer for about 20 minutes, or until vegetables are crisp tender. Add mushrooms and beef. Simmer for about 10 minutes.

Combine cornstarch and water. Stir cornstarch mixture into soup. Continue stirring. Simmer for about 10 minutes, or until soup has thickened. Add salt and pepper to taste.

Makes 4 servings.

# Spinach Soup

4 cups chicken stock
1 medium red-skinned potato,
   peeled and diced
1 small onion, chopped
10-ounce package frozen
   chopped spinach

1/4 teaspoon thyme
1/2 teaspoon salt
salt and pepper to taste
Parmesan cheese, grated

Combine chicken stock, potato, onion, spinach, thyme, and salt in saucepan. Bring to boil. Lower heat. Cover and simmer for about 10 minutes, or until vegetables are tender. Add salt and pepper to taste.

Serve soup in warm tureen or warm individual soup bowls. Garnish with grated Parmesan cheese.

Makes 6 servings.

## ANNIE'S TIPS
Use a small glass jar with a tight lid to combine cornstarch and water; shake well.

# Tomato Bouillon Cup

**2 1/2 cups bouillon**
2 1/2 cups tomato juice
3 lemon slices
2 whole cloves

1 teaspoon chopped fresh basil
1/2 teaspoon sugar
salt and pepper to taste
bread sticks

Combine bouillon, tomato juice, lemon slices, cloves, basil, and sugar in saucepan. Bring to boil. Lower heat. Cover and simmer for about 5 minutes. Add salt and pepper to taste.

Strain soup through fine sieve.

**Serve soup in bouillon cups with bread sticks.**

**Makes 6 servings.**

# Vichyssoise

3 tablespoons salad oil
2 onions, chopped
**2 cups chicken stock**
4 medium potatoes, peeled and
    sliced

1/2 teaspoon salt
2 cups evaporated milk
1 cup yogurt
salt and pepper to taste
snipped chives

Combine salad oil and onion in saucepan. Sauté onion for about 3 minutes. Add chicken stock, potatoes, and salt. Bring to boil. Lower heat. Cover and simmer for about 15 minutes, or until potatoes are tender.

Transfer potato mixture to blender or food processor, in batches if necessary. Blend until smooth.

Transfer potato purée to mixing bowl. Whisk in evaporated milk and yogurt.

Chill soup in covered container for about 4 hours. Add salt and pepper to taste.

Serve soup in chilled bowls. Garnish with snipped chives.

**Makes 6 servings.**

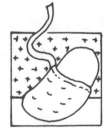

# Chilled Lemon Soup

**1 cup chicken stock**
4 tablespoons lemon juice
1/2 cup cooked rice
1/4 teaspoon salt
1/2 cup yogurt

**3 cups chicken stock**
1 hard-boiled egg, chopped fine
salt and pepper to taste
one strip of lemon peel (avoid
   white pith)

Combine 1 cup chicken stock, lemon juice, rice, and salt in blender or food processor. Blend until smooth. Transfer to mixing bowl. Whisk in yogurt, 3 cups chicken stock, and egg.

Chill soup in covered container for about 4 hours. Add salt and pepper to taste.

Serve in glass bowls. Garnish with strips of lemon peel.

Makes 4 servings.

# Dried Mushroom Soup

1 ounce dried mushrooms,
   rinsed
1 cup warm water
1 onion, sliced
1 stalk celery, sliced
1 carrot, sliced thin

1/4 teaspoon salt
2 tablespoons flour
**5 1/2 cups beef stock**
1 tablespoon pearl barley
1/2 cup cooked white beans
salt and pepper to taste

Combine mushrooms and warm water in large covered saucepan. Set aside for 20 minutes. Put saucepan over heat. Bring to boil. Lower heat. Cover and simmer for about 20 minutes.

Drain mushrooms, reserving liquid. Chop and return to saucepan.

In blender or food processor combine reserved mushroom liquid with onion, celery, carrot, salt, and flour. Blend until smooth.

Transfer purée to saucepan. Add beef stock and barley. Bring mixture to boil. Lower heat. Cover and simmer for about 25 minutes. Stir in cooked white beans. Add salt and pepper to taste.

Serve soup in warm tureen or warm individual soup bowls.

Makes 6 servings.

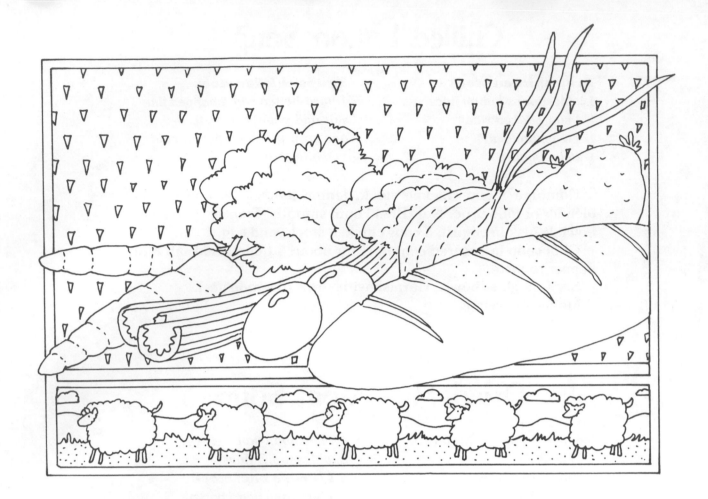

# Lamb and Vegetable Soup

**4 cups lamb stock**
2 carrots, diced
2 stalks celery, diced
1 medium onion, chopped
1 potato, peeled and diced
1/2 teaspoon salt

lamb reserved from stock,
  chopped
3 egg yolks, beaten
1/4 cup lemon juice
1/2 teaspoon paprika
salt to taste

In saucepan combine lamb stock, carrots, celery, onion, and potato. Bring mixture to boil. Lower heat. Cover and simmer for about 10 minutes, or until vegetables are crisp-tender. Add reserved lamb and salt.

In mixing bowl, combine 1 cup hot broth from saucepan, very slowly, with egg yolks. Add lemon juice and paprika to egg yolk mixture. Stir mixture into saucepan. Do not let soup boil. Add salt to taste.

Serve soup in warm tureen with loaf of crusty, warm bread for hearty meal.

**Makes 4 servings.**

Soups

# Chilled Pea Soup

10-ounce package frozen peas,
    broken into chunks
1/2 head lettuce, torn
1 slice onion
1/2 cup cold water

1/2 teaspoon salt
**2 cups cold chicken stock**
1/2 cup sour cream
salt and pepper to taste
2 tablespoons snipped chives

Combine frozen peas, lettuce, onion, water, and salt in blender or food processor. Blend until smooth. Transfer mixture to mixing bowl.

Stir in chicken stock and sour cream. Add salt and pepper to taste.

Serve at once in glass bowls. Garnish with snipped chives.

Makes 4 servings.

# Chilled Lettuce and Watercress Soup

3 tablespoons salad oil
1 small onion
1 bunch watercress (about 2
    cups), reserve 4 sprigs for
    garnish
1 head Boston lettuce, torn
**1/2 cup chicken stock**

2 tablespoons ground almonds
1/2 teaspoon ground nutmeg
1/4 teaspoon salt
**2 cups chicken stock**
1 cup buttermilk or sour milk
salt and pepper to taste
toasted sliced almonds

Combine salad oil and onion in saucepan. Sauté onion for about 2 minutes. Add watercress and lettuce. Stir and cook for about 2 minutes.

Transfer to blender or food processor. Add 1/2 cup chicken stock. Blend until smooth.

Return purée to saucepan. Stir in ground almonds, nutmeg, salt and 2 cups chicken stock. Bring to boil. Lower heat. Cover and simmer for about 5 minutes. Stir in buttermilk.

Chill soup in covered container for about 5 hours. Add salt and pepper to taste.

Serve soup in glass or white bowls. Garnish with watercress sprigs and toasted sliced almonds.

Makes 4 servings.

Soups

# Pear and Leek Soup

4 tablespoons margarine or
    salad oil
2 cups chopped leek
1 pound can pears, packed in
    juice

**4 cups chicken stock**
1/2 teaspoon summer savory
1/4 teaspoon salt
salt and white pepper to taste
croutons

Combine margarine and leek in saucepan. Sauté leek for about 3 minutes, or until tender.

Transfer leek to blender or food processor. Add pears, with juice. Blend until smooth.

Transfer to saucepan. Add chicken stock, summer savory, and salt. Bring to boil. Lower heat. Cover and simmer for about 20 minutes. Add salt and white pepper to taste.

Serve soup in warm tureen or warm individual soup bowls. Garnish with croutons.

Makes 6 servings.

# Chilled Avocado Soup

**1 cup chicken stock**
2 medium avocados, seeded,
    peeled, and cut into chunks
2 tablespoons dry sherry
1/2 teaspoon salt
1 slice onion, chopped

1/4 teaspoon dillweed
1 cup yogurt
**1 cup chicken stock**
salt and pepper to taste
1 small avocado, peeled,
    seeded, and sliced

Combine 1 cup chicken stock, avocado chunks, dry sherry, salt, onion, and dillweed in blender or food processor. Blend until smooth. Transfer to mixing bowl. Stir in yogurt and 1 cup chicken stock.

Chill soup in covered container for about 4 hours. Add salt and pepper to taste.

Serve soup in glass bowls. Garnish with avocado slices.

Makes 4 servings.

# Basil Soup

4 tablespoons margarine
3/4 cup thinly sliced scallions, including green tops
**4 cups chicken stock**
2 tomatoes, peeled, seeded, and chopped

1/2 cup rice
1/2 teaspoon salt
3 cups chopped fresh basil
salt and pepper to taste

Combine margarine and scallions in saucepan. Sauté scallions for about 3 minutes, or until tender. Add chicken stock, tomatoes, and rice. Bring to boil. Lower heat. Cover and simmer for about 20 minutes, or until rice is tender. Add salt and basil. Simmer for about 10 minutes. Add salt and pepper to taste.

Serve soup in warm tureen or warm individual soup bowls.

Makes 4 servings.

# Winter Squash Soup

2 cups water
1 small onion, diced
3 carrots, sliced
1 acorn squash, peeled, seeded, and cut into cubes
1/2 teaspoon salt

**2 cups beef stock**
1 tablespoon lime juice
2 tablespoons honey
1 cup cooked fine noodles
salt and pepper to taste
grated Parmesan cheese

Combine water, onion, carrots, squash, and salt in saucepan. Bring to boil. Lower heat. Cover and simmer for about 15 minutes.

Transfer vegetable mixture to blender or food processor, in batches if necessary. Blend until smooth.

Return the purée to saucepan. Stir in beef stock, lime juice, and honey. Bring to boil. Lower heat. Cover and simmer for about 10 minutes. Stir in noodles. Add salt and pepper to taste.

Serve soup in warm tureen or warm individual soup bowls. Garnish with grated Parmesan cheese.

Makes 4 servings.

Soups

# Scotch Broth

**1 1/2 quarts lamb stock**
1 pound lamb trimmings, fat
   removed
5 tablespoons barley, rinsed
2 carrots, diced
2 onions, diced

2 stalks celery. diced
1 leek, sliced
1 teaspoon salt
salt and pepper to taste
4 tablespoons chopped parsley

Combine lamb stock and lamb trimmings in kettle. Bring mixture to boil. Skim off froth as it rises. Add barley, carrots, onions, celery, leek, and salt. Lower heat. Cover kettle and simmer for about 1 hour and 30 minutes. Add salt and pepper to taste.

Serve soup in warm tureen with loaf of crusty, warm bread for hearty meal. Garnish with chopped parsley.

Makes 6 to 8 servings.

# Consommé with Avocado

3 cups clam juice
**3 cups consommé**

1/3 cup dry sherry
1 small avocado, sliced

Combine clam juice, consommé, and dry sherry in saucepan. Simmer for 2 minutes.

Put 2 or 3 slices of avocado in each warm soup bowl. Pour soup over avocado slices.

Makes 6 servings.

# Chilled Broccoli Chowder

10 ounce package frozen
   chopped broccoli, cooked (do
   not drain)
1 slice onion, chopped
**1 cup chicken stock**
1/2 teaspoon salt

**2 cups chicken stock**
1 cup light cream
2 medium potatoes, peeled,
   diced, and boiled
salt and pepper to taste
grated cheese

Combine broccoli, onion, 1 cup chicken stock, and salt in blender or food processor. Blend until smooth.

ANNIE'S TIPS

Cold soup requires more seasoning than hot soup. Taste-test the soup after chilling.

Pour mixture into mixing bowl. Stir in 2 cups chicken stock, light cream, and potatoes.

Chill soup in covered container for about 4 hours. Add salt and pepper to taste.

Serve soup in glass bowls. Garnish with grated cheese.

Makes 4 servings.

# Cream Sherry Consommé

**2 cups consommé**
1/4 cup dry sherry

2 tablespoons currants or
   raisins
1 1/2 cups light cream

Combine consommé, sherry, and currants in saucepan. Bring to boil. Lower heat and simmer for 5 minutes. Stir in light cream.

Serve at once in warm soup bowls or mugs.

Makes 4 servings.

# Eggplant Soup Parmigiana

3 tablespoons salad oil
1 medium onion, chopped
1 clove garlic, minced (optional)
1 medium eggplant, peeled and
   chopped
**2 cups chicken stock**
1 cup tomato juice

1/2 teaspoon salt
1/4 cup minced parsley
1/2 teaspoon dried thyme,
   crushed
salt and pepper to taste
4–6 ounces Mozzarella cheese,
   shredded

Combine salad oil, onion, and garlic in saucepan. Sauté for about 2 minutes. Add eggplant, chicken stock, tomato juice, salt, parsley, and thyme. Bring to boil. Lower heat. Cover and simmer for about 30 minutes. Add salt and pepper to taste.

Ladle soup into four ovenproof bowls. Top each bowl with portion of cheese. Bake soup in preheated 400 degree oven for about 10 minutes, or until cheese is melted.

Makes 4 servings.

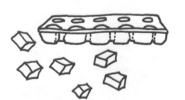

## ANNIE'S TIPS

Rest the glass bowl of soup on a bed of crushed ice, preferably inside a slightly larger glass bowl.

# Cheddar Cheese Soup

1 cup vegetable stock
1 small onion, sliced
2 carrots, sliced
2 tablespoons parsley flakes
3 tablespoons flour
1/4 teaspoon salt
1 cup vegetable stock

2 cups milk
2 cups shredded sharp cheddar
   cheese
dash of cayenne
salt and white pepper to taste
3 tablespoons imitation bacon
   bits

Combine 1 cup vegetable stock, onion, carrots, parsley, flour, and salt in blender or food processor. Blend until smooth.

Transfer to saucepan. Heat mixture. Stir in 1 cup vegetable stock, milk, cheddar cheese, and cayenne. Continue stirring until cheese is melted, about 5 minutes. Add salt and pepper to taste.

Serve soup in warm tureen or warm individual soup bowls. Garnish with imitation bacon bits.

Makes 4 servings.

# Onion Soup

4 tablespoons salad oil
2 pounds onions, sliced thin
2 tablespoons flour
6 cups consommé
1/2 teaspoon paprika
1/2 teaspoon salt

salt and pepper to taste
6 slices French bread, toasted
   with garlic butter
6-8 ounces imported Swiss
   cheese, shredded

Combine salad oil and onions in large saucepan. Sauté onions for about 10 minutes. Stir in flour. Add consommé, paprika, and salt. Bring to boil. Lower heat. Cover and simmer for about 20 minutes. Add salt and pepper to taste.

Transfer soup to six ovenproof bowls. Place one slice of toasted bread on top of each bowl of soup. Top toast with some of shredded cheese.

Place bowls in preheated 400 degree oven for about 10 minutes, or until cheese is melted and golden.

Serve soup at once.

Makes 6 to 8 servings.

# Varied Vegetable Soups

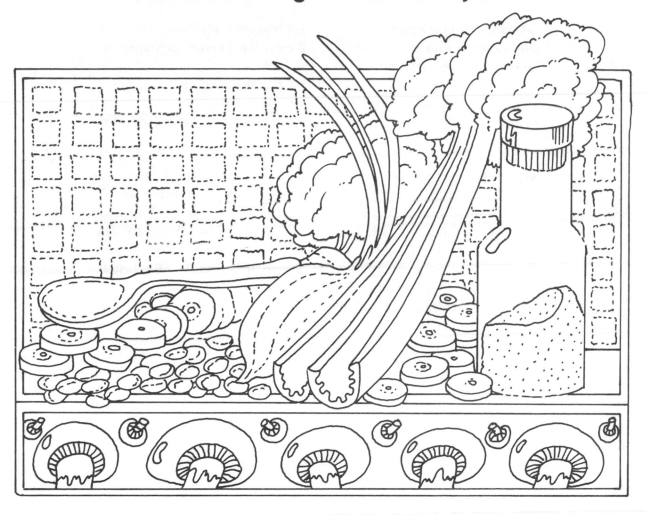

# Vegetable Barley Soup

**4 1/2 cups vegetable stock**
1/2 cup medium barley
1/4 teaspoon crushed dried
  thyme

2 carrots, diced
1 potato, peeled and diced
1 small onion, chopped
salt and pepper to taste

In saucepan combine vegetable stock, barley, and thyme. Bring to boil. Lower heat. Cover and simmer for about 60 minutes. Stir occasionally. Add carrots, potato, and onion.

Cover and simmer for about 20 minutes, or until vegetables and barley are tender. Add salt and pepper to taste.

Serve soup in warm tureen or warm individual soup bowls.

Makes 4 servings.

Soups

# Broccoli and Mushroom Soup

3 tablespoons margarine
1 small onion, minced
10-ounce package frozen
   chopped broccoli
1 cup fresh minced mushrooms
**1 cup vegetable stock**
1/4 teaspoon salt

1/2 teaspoon tarragon, crushed
2 cups light cream or half-and-
   half
1/2 cup dry white wine
salt and pepper to taste
4 fresh mushrooms, sliced thin

Combine margarine and onion in saucepan. Sauté onion for about 3 minutes. Add broccoli, mushrooms, vegetable stock, salt, and tarragon. Bring to boil. Lower heat. Cover and simmer for about 10 minutes. Stir in light cream and wine. Heat to simmer. Do not boil. Add salt and pepper to taste.

Serve soup in warm tureen or warm individual soup bowls. Garnish with sliced mushrooms.

Makes 4 servings.

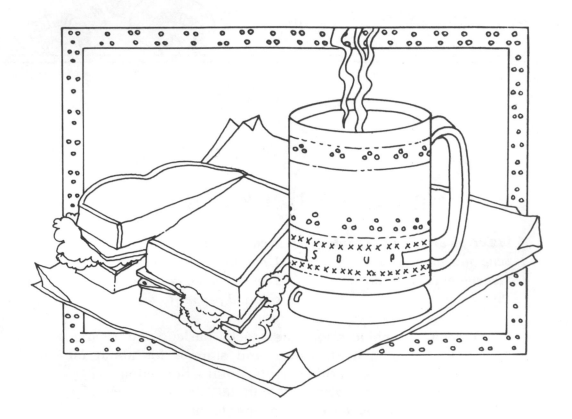

# Brussels Sprout and Cheese Soup

3 tablespoons margarine
1 onion, chopped
2 cups Brussels sprouts,
   trimmed
**1 cup vegetable water**

1/4 teaspoon salt
2 cups milk
1 cup grated cheddar cheese
salt and pepper to taste
croutons

Combine margarine and onion in saucepan. Sauté onion for about 2 minutes. Stir in Brussels sprouts. Continue to sauté for about 3 minutes.

Transfer to blender or food processor. Add vegetable water and salt. Blend until smooth.

Return purée to saucepan. Stir in milk and cheese. Heat to simmer. Stir and simmer for about 5 minutes. Do not boil. Add salt and pepper to taste.

Serve soup in warm tureen or warm individual soup bowls. Garnish with croutons.

Makes 4 servings.

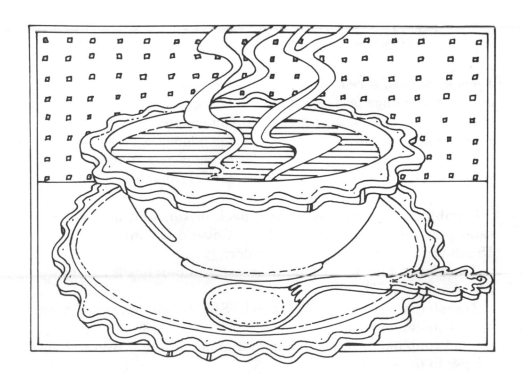

# Vegetable Soup
## with Eggs

1 large onion, chopped
3 tablespoons margarine or
  salad oil
2 cups cauliflower, sliced thin
2 tomatoes, peeled, seeded, and
  chopped
3 carrots, sliced thin
1/3 cup tomato paste

1 large potato, peeled and diced
1 cup peas
**2 cups vegetable water**
2 cups tomato juice
1 teaspoon salt
salt and pepper to taste
4 eggs

In saucepan sauté onion in margarine for about 2 minutes. Add cauliflower, tomatoes, carrots, and tomato paste. Simmer mixture for about 3 minutes. Add potato, peas, vegetable water, tomato juice, and salt. Bring to boil. Lower heat and simmer for about 20 minutes, or until vegetables are just tender. Add salt and pepper to taste.

Carefully add eggs to soup. Cover saucepan and poach eggs until they are set.

Serve at once in warm individual soup bowls with one egg and some vegetables in each bowl.

Makes 4 servings.

# Chilled Orange Carrot Soup

1 pound carrots, sliced
3-inch strip orange peel (avoid
  pith)
1 small onion, sliced
1/2 teaspoon salt
2 cups water

1/4 teaspoon ground ginger
1/4 teaspoon ground cinnamon
1 cup orange juice
1 cup lemon yogurt
salt and pepper to taste
1 carrot, shredded

Combine sliced carrots, orange peel, onion, salt, and water in saucepan. Bring to boil. Lower heat. Cover and simmer for about 15 minutes, or until carrots are tender.

Transfer to blender or food processor, in batches if necessary. Blend until smooth.

Transfer purée to mixing bowl. Stir in ginger, cinnamon, orange juice, and yogurt.

Chill soup in covered container for about 4 hours. Add salt and pepper to taste.

Serve soup in glass bowls. Garnish with shredded carrot.

Makes 4 servings.

# Chilled Green Summer Soup

1 cucumber, sliced
1 avocado, peeled, seeded, and
   cut into chunks
4 scallions, sliced
1/4 teaspoon salt

3 tablespoons lime juice
**1 1/2 cups vegetable water**
1 1/2 cups yogurt
salt and pepper to taste
celery leaves

Combine cucumber, avocado, scallions, salt, and lime juice in blender or food processor. Blend until smooth.

Transfer to mixing bowl. Whisk in vegetable water and yogurt.

Chill soup in covered container for about 4 hours. Add salt and pepper to taste.

Serve soup in glass bowls. Garnish with celery leaves.

Makes 4 servings.

# Chilled Cucumber Soup

1 medium cucumber
2 tablespoons fresh parsley,
   chopped
1/4 cup celery leaves, chopped
1 slice onion, chopped
1 tablespoon snipped dill
1 cup sour milk

1 cup sour cream
1 cup sour milk
1 tablespoon lemon juice
salt to taste
additional sour cream for
   garnish

Cut 4 thin slices from cucumber. Peel the remainder, seed, and cut into chunks.

Combine cucumber chunks in blender or food processor with celery leaves, onion, dill, and 1 cup sour milk. Blend until smooth.

Transfer mixture to mixing bowl. Whisk in sour cream, 1 cup sour milk, lemon juice, and salt.

Chill soup in covered container for about 3 hours.

Serve soup in glass bowls. Garnish with cucumber slices and dollops of sour cream.

Makes 4 servings.

## ANNIE'S TIPS

To prepare sour milk, combine one tablespoon of white vinegar with whole milk to equal 1 cup. Let it stand for 5 minutes.

# Iced Pea Soup

10-ounce package frozen peas
1 medium potato, peeled, cut
  into chunks, and boiled crisp
  tender
1 slice onion, chopped
**1 cup vegetable stock**

1 cup lemon yogurt
**1 cup vegetable stock**
salt and pepper to taste
2 tablespoons chopped fresh
  mint (1 tablespoon dried)

Do not defrost peas. Break frozen peas into chunks. Combine peas, potato, onion, and 1 cup vegetable stock in blender or food processor. Blend until smooth.

Transfer to mixing bowl. Whisk in 1 cup vegetable stock and yogurt. Add salt and pepper to taste.

Serve at once in glass bowls. Garnish with chopped mint.
**Makes 4 servings.**

# Creamy Pea Soup

1 medium potato, peeled,
  sliced, and boiled crisp
  tender
2 cups fresh peas, or 10-ounce
  package frozen peas
**3/4 cup vegetable water**
2 tablespoons salad oil
1 tablespoon fresh snipped
  parsley

1/2 teaspoon dried thyme
1 slice onion
**1 cup vegetable water**
salt and pepper to taste
1 cup sour cream
1/4 pound fresh mushrooms,
  sliced thin

Combine potato, fresh or frozen peas, 3/4 cup vegetable water, salad oil, parsley, thyme, and onion in blender or food processor. Blend until smooth. Transfer mixure to saucepan. Stir in 1 cup vegetable water. Simmer mixture for 5 minutes. Add salt and pepper to taste. Whisk in sour cream.

Serve soup in warm tureen. Garnish with sliced mushrooms.
**Makes 4 servings.**

ANNIE'S TIPS
Sprinkle dried herbs with water 10 minutes
before using.

# Mushroom Barley Soup

1 cup water
1 small onion, sliced
1 medium potato, peeled and
  sliced thin
1/3 cup fine barley
2 tablespoons dried mushroom
  flakes, rinsed

**5 cups vegetable stock**
1/4 teaspoon salt
1/8 teaspoon pepper
1/4 cup pastina
salt and pepper to taste
sour cream
snipped chives

Combine water, onion, and potato in blender or food processor. Blend until smooth.

Transfer purée to saucepan. Add barley, dried mushrooms, vegetable stock, salt, and pepper. Bring to boil. Lower heat. Cover and simmer for about 1 hour and 15 minutes, or until barley is tender. Stir in pastina. Cover and simmer for about 20 minutes. Add salt and pepper to taste.

Serve soup in warm tureen or warm individual soup bowls. Garnish with dollop of sour cream and snipped chives.

**Makes 4 servings.**

# Chilled Tomato and Vegetable Soup

1 pound tomatoes, canned or
  fresh
4 medium carrots, sliced
2 stalks celery, chopped
1/2 medium green pepper,
  chopped
1 tablespoon chopped fresh
  basil

1 small onion, chopped
1/2 tablespoon chopped fresh
  thyme
**2 cups vegetable stock**
1 cup orange juice
1/4 teaspoon salt
salt and pepper to taste
slivers of orange peel

Combine tomatoes, carrots, celery, green pepper, onion, basil, and thyme in blender or food processor. Blend until smooth.

Transfer to mixing bowl. Stir in vegetable stock, orange juice, and salt.

Chill soup in covered container for about 4 hours. Add salt and pepper to taste.

Serve soup in glass bowls. Garnish with orange peel.

**Makes 4 to 6 servings.**

ANNIE'S TIPS
When substituting dried herbs for fresh, use half the amount suggested here.

Soups

# Dilled Potato and Onion Soup

4 large potatoes, peeled and
  diced
1 onion, chopped
2 cloves garlic, minced (optional)
1/2 teaspoon salt

**3 cups vegetable water**
1 cup milk
1/2 cup snipped dill
salt and pepper to taste
3 tablespoons imitation bacon
  bits

Combine potatoes, onion, garlic, salt, and vegetable water in saucepan. Bring mixture to boil. Lower heat. Cover and simmer for about 15 minutes. With slotted spoon remove half cooked potatoes from saucepan. Combine potatoes with milk in blender or food processor. Blend until smooth. Add potato purée and dill to saucepan. Simmer for about 5 minutes. Add salt and pepper to taste.

Serve soup in warm tureen or warm individual soup bowls. Garnish with imitation bacon bits.

**Makes 4 servings.**

Soups

# Corn Chowder

1 large potato, peeled and sliced
1 cup water
1 small onion, sliced
1/2 teaspoon salt
2 tablespoons melted margarine or salad oil

2 tablespoons flour
3 cups cooked corn, fresh or canned
**1 cup vegetable water**
2 cups milk
salt and pepper to taste
cheese croutons

Combine potato, water, onion, and salt in covered saucepan. Bring mixture to boil. Lower heat. Cover and simmer until vegetables are crisp tender, about 10 minutes.

Transfer potato mixture to blender or food processor. Add melted margarine and flour. Blend until smooth.

Return potato purée to saucepan. Bring mixture to boil. Lower heat and stir in corn, vegetable water, and milk. Add salt and pepper to taste. Heat to simmer.

Serve soup at once in warm tureen or warm individual soup bowls. Garnish with cheese croutons.

**Makes 4 servings.**

# Cold Beet and Cucumber Soup

3 cups buttermilk or sour milk
1 cup sour cream
1-pound can beets, chopped (do not drain)
1 cup cucumber, peeled, seeded, and chopped
1 tablespoon snipped dill

2 tablespoons minced scallions
1/2 teaspoon salt
3 tablespoons lemon juice
3 tablespoons sugar
3 hard-boiled eggs, chopped
salt and pepper to taste
sour cream garnish

In mixing bowl whisk together milk and sour cream. Stir in beets, cucumbers, dill, scallions, and salt. In small bowl combine lemon juice and sugar. Stir lemon juice mixture into milk mixture. Add eggs.

Chill soup in covered container for about 5 hours. Add salt and pepper to taste.

Serve soup in glass bowls. Garnish with dollops of sour cream.

**Makes 6 servings.**

Soups

# Cool Cucumber and Red Onion Soup

1 tablespoon snipped dill
1/4 teaspoon salt
1/8 teaspoon white pepper
2 medium cucumbers, peeled
    and sliced thin
2 red onions, sliced thin
2 tablespoons snipped dill

additional salt
2 cups sour cream
1 tablespoon honey
2 tablespoons lemon juice
salt and pepper to taste
snipped dill

Combine 1 tablespoon snipped dill, 1/4 teaspoon salt, and white pepper in crock or saucepan. Place one quarter of sliced cucumber on top, then one quarter of sliced onions. Do not mix. Sprinkle salt and about 1/2 tablespoon snipped dill over layered vegetables.

Repeat layers using all vegetables and dill. Lightly sprinkle salt over each layer.

Combine sour cream and honey. Spread sour cream mixture on top layer.

Cover and chill for about 8 hours. Stir in lemon juice. Add salt and pepper to taste.

Serve soup in glass bowls. Garnish with snipped dill.

Makes 4 servings.

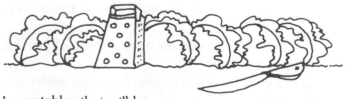

ANNIE'S TIPS

Chopped or shredded vegetables that will be added to soup need to be cooked only briefly. This method retains their food value.

# Red Bean Soup with Rice

**5 cups vegetable water**
1/2 cup long grain rice
1/4 teaspoon salt
4 cups water

1/2 pound red kidney beans
1/4 teaspoon salt
salt and pepper to taste
honey

Combine 5 cups vegetable water, rice, and salt in saucepan. Bring to boil. Lower heat. Cover and simmer for about 1 hour and 30 minutes.

At same time, combine 4 cups water, red kidney beans, and salt in separate saucepan. Bring to boil. Lower heat. Cover and simmer for about 1 hour and 30 minutes.

Combine rice and beans in one large saucepan. Stir and blend. Simmer mixture, stirring occasionally, for about 40 minutes. Soup will be very thick. Add salt and pepper to taste.

Serve in warm individual soup bowls, with honey drizzled on top.

Makes 6 servings.

# Chilled Artichoke Soup with Endive

9-ounce package frozen
　artichoke hearts
1 cup water
1/2 teaspoon salt
2 tablespoons margarine
1/2 pound endive, trimmed and
　torn
1 small onion, sliced

1/2 teaspoon sugar
1 egg yolk
1 cup light cream or half-and-
　half
**2 cups vegetable stock**
salt and pepper to taste
torn endive

Combine artichokes, water, salt, and margarine in saucepan. Bring to boil. Lower heat. Cover and simmer for about 8 minutes.

Transfer to blender or food processor. Add endive, onion, and sugar. Blend until smooth. Add egg yolk and blend.

Transfer purée to mixing bowl. Stir in light cream and vegetable stock.

Chill soup in covered container for about 4 hours. Add salt and pepper to taste.

Serve soup in chilled bowls. Garnish with torn endive.

**Makes 6 servings.**

Soups

# Iced Green Bean Soup

10-ounce package frozen green
  beans
1 cup tomato juice
2 tablespoons fresh chopped
  basil
1 slice onion

1/2 teaspoon salt
1 egg yolk
1 cup tomato juice
2 cups sour milk
salt and pepper to taste
parsley sprigs

Combine green beans, 1 cup tomato juice, basil, onion, and salt in a blender or food processor. Blend until smooth. Add egg yolk.

Transfer to mixing bowl. Stir in 1 cup tomato juice and sour milk. Add salt and pepper to taste.

Serve soup at once in glass bowls. Garnish with sprigs of parsley.

**Makes 4 servings.**

Soups

# Chilled Golden Squash Soup

2 yellow summer squash, sliced
3 tomatoes, cut into eighths,
    and cored
1 small onion, sliced
1 small green pepper, seeded
    and diced
1/4 teaspoon dried thyme

1/4 teaspoon dried basil
1 teaspoon salt
**2 cups vegetable stock**
1 cup orange juice
salt and freshly ground pepper
    to taste
snipped parsley

Combine squash, tomatoes, onion, green pepper, thyme, basil, and salt in blender or food processor. Blend until smooth.

Transfer to mixing bowl. Stir in vegetable stock and orange juice.

Chill in covered container for about 4 hours. Add salt and pepper to taste.

Serve in glass bowls. Garnish with parsley.

Makes 6 servings.

# Chilled Cauliflower Soup

10 ounces frozen cauliflower
**1 cup vegetable water**
1 medium potato, peeled and
    sliced thin
1 slice onion, diced

1/4 teaspoon salt
2 cups buttermilk or sour milk
salt and pepper to taste
chopped fresh chives

Remove cauliflower from the freezer. Separate frozen florets.

Combine vegetable water, potato, and onion in saucepan. Bring to boil. Lower heat. Cover and simmer for about 5 minutes, or until just tender.

Transfer vegetable mixture to blender or food processor. Add cauliflower and salt. Blend until smooth.

Transfer purée to mixing bowl. Whisk in buttermilk. Chill in covered container for about 4 hours. Add salt and pepper to taste.

Serve soup in glass bowls. Garnish with chopped fresh chives.

Makes 4 servings.

# Cream of Mushroom Soup

1 pound mushrooms, soaked,
    wiped, and trimmed
**3 cups vegetable stock,** heated
    in saucepan
**1 cup vegetable stock**
2 scallions, sliced

1 medium potato, peeled,
    sliced, and boiled crisp
    tender
1/2 teaspoon salt
freshly ground pepper to taste
3 egg yolks
1 cup evaporated milk

Reserve 6 mushrooms for garnish.

Combine 1 cup vegetable stock, mushrooms, scallions, potato, salt, and pepper in blender or food processor. Blend until smooth. Add mixture to hot stock in saucepan. Simmer for 5 minutes. Whisk egg yolks in mixing bowl. Whisk evaporated milk into egg yolks. Whisk continuously while adding 1 cup hot mixture from saucepan. Stir this mixture into saucepan. Cook over medium heat, stirring continuously, until soup is very hot. Do not boil.

Slice reserved mushrooms. Add mushrooms to soup. Add salt and pepper to taste.

Serve soup in warm tureen or warm individual soup bowls.

**Makes 6 servings.**

Soups

# Rice Soup

2 tablespoons salad oil
1 small onion, diced
6-ounce package seasoned long
    grain and wild rice
**3 cups vegetable water**

**3 cups vegetable stock**
1 cup tomatoes, crushed
2 tablespoons dried mushroom
    flakes, rinsed
salt and pepper to taste

Combine salad oil and onion in large saucepan. Sauté onion for about 2 minutes. Add seasoned rice, vegetable water, vegetable stock, tomatoes, and dried mushrooms. Bring to boil. Lower heat. Cover and simmer for about 30 minutes. Add salt and pepper to taste.

Serve soup in warm tureen or warm individual soup bowls.

Makes 6 servings.

# Sweet Potato Soup

1 onion, chopped
3 tablespoons margarine or
    salad oil
3 tomatoes, peeled, seeded, and
    chopped
2 tablespoons chopped fresh
    parsley
1 pound sweet potatoes, peeled
    and sliced

1 cup sour milk
**1 quart vegetable stock or
    vegetable water**
1/4 cup cold water
2 tablespoons cornstarch
salt and pepper to taste
1/4 cup shredded coconut

In saucepan sauté onion in margarine for about 2 minutes. Add tomatoes and parsley. Simmer mixture over low heat for about 5 minutes. Add sweet potatoes. Cover and simmer for about 5 minutes. In blender or food processor combine vegetable mixture with sour milk. Blend until smooth. Reserve purée. Pour vegetable stock into saucepan. Heat to boil. Combine water and cornstarch. Lower heat to simmer. Stir in cornstarch mixture. Continue stirring until stock has thickened slightly. Stir in purée. Cover and simmer for about 5 minutes. Do not boil. Add salt and pepper to taste.

Serve soup in warm tureen or warm individual soup bowls. Garnish with shredded coconut.

Makes 4 servings.

# Chilled Celery Soup

4 cups vegetable water
4 stalks celery, with tops, sliced
1 onion, sliced
1/4 teaspoon thyme
4 sprigs parsley
1 bay leaf
1/4 cup rice

1/2 teaspoon celery salt
3 eggs, beaten
2 tablespoons lemon juice
salt and white pepper to taste
1 lemon, sliced thin
celery leaves

Combine vegetable water, celery, onion, thyme, parsley, bay leaf, rice, and celery salt in large saucepan. Bring to boil. Lower heat. Cover and simmer for about 25 minutes.

Remove bay leaf. Strain through fine sieve over mixing bowl. Transfer cooked vegetable mixture to blender or food processor. Add 1 cup of reserved liquid. Blend until smooth. Transfer purée to mixing bowl containing reserved liquid.

Combine eggs and lemon juice in separate mixing bowl. Beat until light and fluffy. Whisk egg mixture into vegetable mixture.

Chill soup in covered container for about 4 hours. Add salt and pepper to taste.

Serve soup in glass or white bowls. Garnish with lemon slices and top with celery leaves.

Makes 6 servings.

# Creamed Spinach Soup

2 tablespoons salad oil
1 small onion, chopped
2 cups vegetable stock
9 or 10-ounce package frozen
    creamed spinach (removed
    from pouch)

1 cup light cream or half-and-half
salt and pepper to taste

Combine salad oil and onion in saucepan. Sauté onion for about 2 minutes.

Add vegetable stock and spinach. Stir and bring to simmer. Lower heat. Cover and simmer for about 10 minutes. Stir in light cream. Heat to simmer. Do not boil. Add salt and pepper to taste.

Serve in warm tureen or warm individual soup bowls.

Makes 4 servings.

# Celery Cabbage Soup

*2 cups vegetable water* or
    *green vegetable stock*
*2 tablespoons salad oil*
*1 onion, diced*
*2 tablespoons salad oil*
*1 stalk celery, with top, sliced*

*1 bunch celery cabbage, sliced*
*1/4 cup cooked rice*
*1/2 teaspoon celery salt*
*2 cups yogurt or sour cream*
*salt and white pepper to taste*
*minced parsley*

Combine 2 tablespoons salad oil and onion in saucepan. Sauté onion for about 2 minutes. Add 2 tablespoons salad oil, celery, and celery cabbage. Stir and sauté mixture for about 5 minutes.

Transfer to blender or food processor. Add rice and celery salt. Blend until smooth.

Return purée to saucepan. Stir in yogurt and vegetable water. Heat soup to simmer. Do not boil. Add salt and pepper to taste.

Serve soup in warm tureen or warm individual white soup bowls. Garnish with minced parsley.

Makes 6 servings.

Soups

# Chilled Avocado and Watercress Soup

2 avocados, seeded, peeled,
  and cut into chunks
1 bunch watercress, about 2
  cups, reserve 4 sprigs for garnish
**1 cup vegetable water**
1 tablespoon chopped scallions

2 parsley sprigs
1/4 teaspoon salt
2 cups yogurt
2 tablespoons lemon juice
dash cayenne
salt to taste
chopped watercress leaves

Combine avocados, watercress, vegetable water, scallions, parsley and salt in blender or food processor. Blend until smooth.

Transfer purée to mixing bowl. Whisk in yogurt, lemon juice, and cayenne. Chill soup in covered container for about 2 hours. Add salt to taste.

Serve soup in glass or white bowls. Garnish with chopped watercress leaves.

Makes 4 servings.

# Vegetable Chowder

2 tablespoons salad oil
1 onion, diced
**4 cups vegetable water**
2 carrots, sliced
2 stalks celery, diced
2 medium zucchini, cubed
1 cup green beans, snapped
2 tomatoes, peeled, seeded, and
chopped

2 potatoes, peeled and diced
1/2 teaspoon salt
1/2 teaspoon thyme
1/2 teaspoon marjoram
2 tablespoons quick-cooking
farina
1/2 cup light cream
salt and pepper to taste
minced parsley

Combine salad oil and onion in saucepan. Sauté onion for about 3 minutes. Add vegetable water, carrots, celery, zucchini, green beans, tomatoes, potatoes, salt, thyme, marjoram, and farina. Bring to boil. Lower heat. Cover and simmer for about 15 minutes, or until vegetables are tender. Stir in light cream. Add salt and pepper to taste.

Serve soup in warm tureen or warm individual soup bowls. Garnish with minced parsley.

Makes 6 servings.

# Tomato Rice Soup

2 tablespoons salad oil
1 onion, chopped
**1 cup vegetable water**
2 carrots, sliced
1/4 teaspoon salt
1/4 teaspoon basil
1/4 teaspoon parsley flakes
**2 1/2 cups vegetable stock**

1/4 cup rice
1 pound tomatoes, peeled,
seeded, and chopped (about
1 1/2 cups)
2 tablespoons tomato paste
1 tablespoon honey
salt and white pepper to taste
minced basil

Combine salad oil and onion in saucepan. Sauté onion for about 3 minutes. Add vegetable water and carrots. Bring to boil. Lower heat. Cover and simmer for about 10 minutes.

Transfer mixture to blender or food processor. Add salt, basil, and parsley. Blend until smooth.

Return purée to saucepan. Add vegetable stock, rice, tomatoes, tomato paste, and honey. Bring to boil. Lower heat. Cover and simmer for about 25 minutes, or until rice is tender. Add salt and pepper to taste.

Serve soup at once in warm tureen or warm individual soup bowls. Garnish with minced basil.

Makes 4 servings.

# Pumpkin Soup

2 tablespoons salad oil
1 small onion, minced
1 stalk celery, minced
1-pound can or 2 cups cooked
 pumpkin, cubed
**2 cups vegetable stock**
2 tablespoons honey

1/2 teaspoon salt
1/4 teaspoon nutmeg
1 cup light cream or evaporated
 milk
salt and pepper to taste
minced parsley

Combine salad oil, onion, and celery in saucepan. Sauté for about 3 minutes. Add pumpkin, vegetable stock, honey, salt, and nutmeg. Bring to boil. Lower heat. Cover and simmer for about 10 minutes. Slowly stir in light cream. Add salt and pepper to taste. Heat to simmer. Do not boil.

Serve soup in warm tureen or warm individual soup bowls. Garnish with minced parsley.

Makes 4 servings.

# Chilled Blue Cheese Soup with Caviar

2 ounces blue cheese, crumbled
1 cup milk
1/4 teaspoon dried chives
1/4 teaspoon dried thyme
1/8 teaspoon white pepper

2 cups sour cream or yogurt
additional milk, if desired
salt and pepper to taste
4-ounce jar red caviar

Combine blue cheese, milk, chives, thyme, and pepper in blender or food processor. Blend until smooth.

Transfer to mixing bowl. Whisk in sour cream. Check consistency and add more milk if desired. Chill in covered container for about 6 hours. Add salt and pepper to taste.

Serve soup in glass or white bowls. Garnish each serving with dollop of caviar.

Makes 4 servings.

# Alfalfa Sprout Soup with Mushrooms

**4 cups vegetable stock**
1 tablespoon soy sauce
1/4 pound mushrooms, soaked, wiped, and sliced very thin
1 cup alfalfa sprouts

1/4 cup cooked shrimp, minced (optional)
salt and pepper to taste
2 tablespoons minced parsley

Combine vegetable stock, soy sauce, and mushrooms in saucepan. Bring to boil. Lower heat. Cover and simmer for about 3 minutes. Add sprouts. Cover and simmer for about 2 minutes. Stir in cooked shrimp. Add salt and pepper to taste.

Serve soup at once in warm tureen or warm individual soup bowls. Garnish with minced parsley.

Makes 4 servings.

# Corn Soup

**3 cups vegetable stock**
8 or 9-ounce can cream style corn
1/2 teaspoon salt
2 tablespoons cornstarch
**3 tablespoons vegetable stock or water**

2 egg whites, beaten until frothy
2 tablespoons milk
salt and pepper to taste
minced parsley or alfalfa sprouts

Heat vegetable stock in saucepan to boil. Lower heat to simmer.

Combine corn and salt in blender or food processor. Blend until smooth.

Combine cornstarch and vegetable stock. Set aside. Combine egg whites and milk. Set aside.

Soups

Add puréed corn to saucepan. Increase heat. Stir continuously until mixture comes to boil. Lower heat slightly. Stir in cornstarch mixture. Continue to stir until mixture thickens. Add salt and pepper to taste.

Remove saucepan from heat. Without stirring, pour egg white mixture into saucepan very slowly. Stir once.

Serve soup in warm tureen or warm individual soup bowls. Garnish with parsley or sprouts.

Makes 4 servings.

# Mushroom Bisque

3 tablespoons margarine or
  salad oil
3/4 pound mushrooms, soaked,
  wiped, and sliced
1 tablespoon flour
2 cups heated clam juice

1/2 cup half-and-half or
  evaporated milk
1 tablespoon dry sherry
1/4 pound mushrooms, soaked,
  wiped, and sliced very thin
salt and pepper to taste
minced parsley

Combine margarine and 3/4 pound mushrooms in saucepan. Sauté mushrooms for about 2 minutes. Stir in flour until blended. Stir in clam juice. Bring to boil. Lower heat. Cover and simmer for about 5 minutes.

Transfer mixture, in batches if necessary, to blender or food processor. Blend until smooth.

Transfer purée to saucepan. Stir in half-and-half, dry sherry, and 1/4 pound mushrooms. Simmer bisque for about 5 minutes. Do not boil. Add salt and pepper to taste.

Serve bisque in warm tureen or warm individual soup bowls. Garnish with minced parsley.

Makes 4 servings.

# Herbed Spinach Soup

3 cups basic fish stock
2 tablespoons salad oil
1 onion, diced
1 tablespoon flour
1 cup clam juice
10-ounce package frozen
  chopped spinach

1/4 teaspoon salt
2 tablespoons parsley flakes
1/4 teaspoon tarragon
salt and pepper to taste
grated lemon rind

Combine salad oil and onion in saucepan. Sauté onion for about 2 minutes. Stir in flour. Add basic fish stock and clam juice. Bring to boil. Add frozen spinach, salt, parsley flakes, and tarragon. Return to boil. Lower heat. Cover and simmer for about 15 minutes. Add salt and pepper to taste.

Serve soup in warm tureen or warm individual soup bowls. Garnish with grated lemon rind.

Makes 4 servings.

# Strips of Cucumber Soup

| | |
|---|---|
| 1 tablespoon dried mushroom flakes, rinsed | 1 medium cucumber |
| | 1 tablespoon soy sauce |
| **4 cups vegetable stock, warm** | salt and pepper to taste |

Combine dried mushrooms and vegetable stock in saucepan. Set aside for about 30 minutes.

Peel cucumber and cut into quarters lengthwise. Remove seeds. Slice vertically in julienne strips. Set aside.

Add soy sauce to mushroom and stock mixture. Heat to boil. Lower heat. Cover and simmer for about 2 minutes. Add cucumber. Cover and simmer for about 2 minutes. Add salt and pepper to taste.

Serve soup at once in warm tureen or warm individual soup bowls.

Makes 4 servings.

# Schav

| | |
|---|---|
| 1 pound schav (sorrel, sour grass), washed | sugar or lemon juice to taste |
| | 2 eggs |
| 1/2 onion, grated | 1 cup sour cream |
| 6 cups water | salt and pepper to taste |
| 1 teaspoon salt | 1 hard-boiled egg, minced |
| 1 tablespoon lemon juice | sour cream |
| 2 tablespoons sugar | |

Combine schav, onion, water, and salt in large saucepan. Bring to boil. Lower heat. Cover and simmer for about 1 hour.

Combine lemon juice and sugar. Add to saucepan. Continue to simmer for about 15 minutes. Add either sugar or lemon juice to taste. Remove saucepan from heat.

Beat eggs in mixing bowl. Stirring constantly, slowly add 1 cup hot soup. Stir in 1 cup sour cream. Stir mixture into saucepan.

Chill soup in covered container for about 5 hours. Add salt and pepper to taste.

Serve soup in glass bowls. Garnish with minced egg and sour cream.

Makes 6 servings.

# Split Pea Soup

**5 cups vegetable water** and/or
    **vegetable stock**
1 cup split peas
1 carrot, diced
1 onion, diced

1 stalk celery, diced
1/2 teaspoon salt
1/4 cup pastina
salt and pepper to taste
minced parsley

Combine vegetable water, split peas, carrot, onion, celery, and salt in large saucepan. Bring to boil. Lower heat. Cover and simmer for about 2 hours. Stir occasionally. Add pastina. Cover and simmer for about 15 minutes. Add salt and pepper to taste.

Serve soup in warm tureen or warm individual soup bowls. Garnish with minced parsley.

Makes 4 servings.

# Hearty Vegetable Soup

**4 cups vegetable stock**
1 onion, chopped
3 tablespoons parsley, minced
2 carrots, diced
2 stalks celery and tops,
    chopped
2 potatoes, peeled and diced
2 zucchinis, diced

1/2 pound mushrooms, soaked,
    wiped, trimmed, and
    chopped
1 bay leaf (optional)
1/2 teaspoon salt
2 tablespoons cornstarch
1/4 cup water
salt and pepper to taste

In saucepan combine vegetable stock, onion, parsley, carrots, celery, potato, zucchini, mushrooms, bay leaf, and salt. Bring mixture to boil. Lower heat. Cover and simmer for about 20 minutes. Remove bay leaf. Combine cornstarch and water. Stir cornstarch mixture into saucepan. Continue stirring until soup has thickened slightly. Add salt and pepper to taste.

Serve soup in warm tureen or warm individual soup bowls.

Makes 4 servings.

# Seafood Soups

# Red Cod Chowder

2 tablespoons salad oil
1 onion minced
**6 cups puréed fish stock**
2 cups water
3 medium potatoes, peeled and
   cubed

1/2 teaspoon salt
2 pounds codfish filets,
   cut into strips
1 tablespoon lemon juice
salt and pepper to taste

Combine salad oil and onions in large saucepan. Sauté onions for about 2 minutes, or until just tender. Add puréed fish stock, water, potatoes, and salt. Bring to boil. Lower heat. Cover and simmer for about 10 minutes. Add fish and lemon juice. Cover and simmer for about 10 minutes, or until potatoes are tender. Add salt and pepper to taste.

Serve soup in warm tureen or warm individual soup bowls.
**Makes 4 servings.**

# Shrimp Gumbo

**2 cups basic fish stock**
3 tablespoons salad oil
1 onion, diced
1/2 green pepper, diced
2 cups sliced okra, fresh or
   frozen
2 stalks celery, sliced

2 1/2 cups water
1 teaspoon salt
3/4 pound small shrimp, peeled
   and de-veined
1 cup cooked rice
salt and pepper to taste

Combine salad oil, onion, and green pepper in large saucepan. Sauté for about 3 minutes, or until just tender. Add okra, celery, water, and salt. Bring to boil. Lower heat. Cover and simmer for about 10 minutes. Stir in shrimp and basic fish stock. Cover and simmer for about 5 minutes. Stir in cooked rice. Add salt and pepper to taste.

Serve soup at once in warm tureen or warm individual soup bowls.

Makes 6 servings.

# Vegetable Clam Chowder

1 cup clam juice
1 cup water
8-ounce can tomato sauce
1-pound can tomatoes
2 medium potatoes, diced
1 green pepper, diced
2 carrots, diced
2 onions, diced
2 stalks celery, diced
1 tablespoon marjoram

1 teaspoon thyme
1/2 teaspoon salt
1/4 teaspoon pepper
1 teaspoon sugar
14–16 ounces canned minced
   clams
1 cup corn, fresh or frozen
salt and pepper to taste
chopped parsley

Combine clam juice, water, tomato sauce, tomatoes, potatoes, green pepper, carrots, onions, celery, marjoram, thyme, salt, pepper, and sugar in large saucepan. Bring to boil. Lower heat. Cover and simmer for about 20 minutes, or until vegetables are crisp tender. Add minced clams and corn. Simmer soup for about 10 minutes. Add salt and pepper to taste.

Serve soup in warm tureen or warm individual soup bowls. Garnish with chopped parsley.

Makes 6 servings.

# Shrimp and Crab Soup

**1 cup basic fish stock**
1/4 cup onion, minced
1 stalk celery, minced
3 tablespoons flour
1 teaspoon salt
4 tablespoons margarine

1 quart milk
6 ounces frozen crabmeat
6 ounces frozen or fresh tiny
  shrimp
salt and white pepper to taste
chopped parsley

Combine margarine, onion, and celery in large saucepan. Sauté for about 3 minutes. Stir in flour and salt. Stir in basic fish stock and milk. Stir continuously until mixture thickens. Do not boil.

Add crabmeat and shrimp. Heat soup to simmer. Simmer for about 10 minutes. Do not boil. Add salt and white pepper to taste.

Serve soup in warm tureen or warm individual soup bowls. Garnish with chopped parsley.

Makes 6 servings.

Soups

# Clam and Mushroom Soup

4 tablespoons margarine or
   salad oil
1/2 pound mushrooms, soaked,
   wiped, and sliced thin
3 tablespoons flour
2 cups clam juice
7–7 1/2 ounces canned or fresh
   minced clams

1 cup evaporated milk or light
   cream
1/2 teaspoon salt
1/4 teaspoon ground white pepper
1/8 teaspoon tarragon
salt and pepper to taste
ground paprika

Combine margarine with mushrooms in saucepan. Sauté mushrooms for about 5 minutes. Stir in flour. Stir in clam juice and minced clams. Continue stirring mixture until slightly thickened. Stir in evaporated milk, salt, pepper, and tarragon. Heat to just under boil. Do not boil. Add salt and pepper to taste.

Serve soup in warm tureen or warm individual soup bowls. Garnish with sprinkle of paprika.

**Makes 4 servings.**

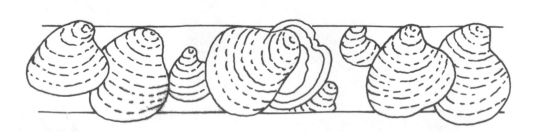

# Chilled Shrimp Bisque

3/4 **cup basic fish stock** or
    cooking water from shrimp
2 tablespoons salad oil
1 small onion, diced
1 stalk celery and top, diced
14–16 ounces shrimp, cooked,
    peeled, de-veined, and sliced if
    large
1/4 teaspoon paprika

1/2 teaspoon salt
2 tablespoons flour
1 cup evaporated milk
3 cups milk
2–3 dashes cayenne
salt to taste
alfalfa sprouts or minced
    parsley

Combine salad oil, onion, and celery in saucepan. Sauté vegetables for about 3 minutes, or until just tender.

Transfer to blender or food processor. Add shrimp, basic fish stock, paprika, salt, and flour. Blend. Add evaporated milk. Blend until smooth.

Transfer to mixing bowl. Stir in milk and cayenne.

Chill soup in covered container for about 4 hours. Add salt to taste.

Serve bisque in glass bowls. Garnish with alfalfa sprouts or minced parsley.

**Makes 6 servings.**

# Crab Gumbo

2 **cups basic fish stock**
4 tablespoons margarine or
    salad oil
1 small onion, sliced
1/4 cup minced green pepper
1/4 cup raw rice
3 medium tomatoes, peeled and
    diced

1 cup sliced okra
6–7 ounces crabmeat, flaked
1/2 teaspoon Worcestershire
    sauce
salt and pepper to taste
parsley sprigs

Combine margarine, onion, and green pepper in large saucepan. Sauté for about 5 minutes. Add basic fish stock and rice. Bring to boil. Lower heat. Cover and simmer for about 20 minutes. Stir in tomatoes, okra, crabmeat, and Worcestershire sauce. Simmer soup for about 20 minutes. Add salt and pepper to taste.

Serve soup in warm tureen or warm individual soup bowls. Garnish with parsley sprigs.

**Makes 6 servings.**

Soups

# Chilled Lobster Bisque

2 tablespoons salad oil
1 stalk celery, with top, diced
1/2 green pepper, diced
1 onion, diced
1 cup tomato juice
3-ounce package cream cheese
   and chives, softened
1/4 teaspoon salt

1 whole pimiento, cut into
   chunks
dash cayenne
4 ounces cooked lobster,
   minced
2 cups sour cream or yogurt
salt and cayenne to taste
snipped chives

Combine salad oil, celery, green pepper, and onion in saucepan. Sauté mixture for about 5 minutes.

Transfer to blender or food processor. Add tomato juice, cream cheese, salt, pimiento, and cayenne. Blend until smooth.

Transfer purée to mixing bowl. Whisk in lobster and sour cream.

Chill soup in covered container for about 3 hours. Add salt and cayenne to taste.

Serve soup in white or glass bowls. Garnish with snipped chives.

Makes 4 servings.

# Clam Bisque

4 tablespoons margarine or
   salad oil
1 small onion, minced
1 stalk celery, minced
4 tablespoons flour
1/2 teaspoon salt
dash cayenne
1/8 teaspoon dry mustard

2 teaspoons lemon rind
2 cups milk
14–16 ounces canned or fresh
   minced clams
2 cups milk
salt and pepper to taste
chopped parsley

Combine margarine, onion, and celery in saucepan. Sauté for about 5 minutes or until vegetables are tender. Stir in flour, salt, cayenne, dry mustard, and lemon rind. Slowly stir in 2 cups milk. Continue stirring until mixture has thickened slightly.

Combine 2 cups milk with minced clams in separate saucepan. Heat to simmer. Do not boil. Stir milk and clam mixture into first saucepan. Add salt and pepper to taste.

Serve bisque in warm tureen or warm individual soup bowls. Garnish with chopped parsley.

Makes 4 servings.

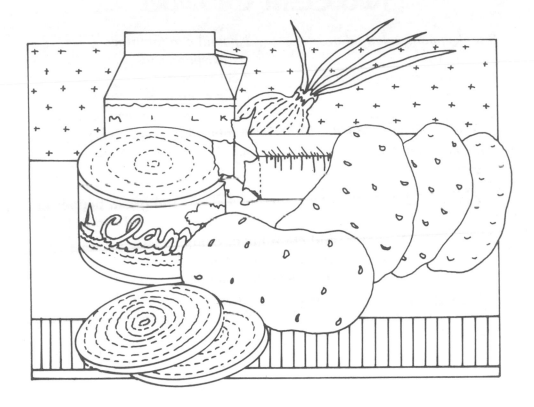

# White Clam Chowder

2 tablespoons margarine or
  salad oil
1 onion, diced
2 medium potatoes, peeled and
  diced
1 cup clam juice

water
14–16 ounces canned or fresh
  minced clams
2 cups half-and-half or light
  cream
salt and pepper to taste

Combine margarine and onion in saucepan. Sauté onion for about 3 minutes. Add potatoes, clam juice, and enough water to cover potatoes. Bring to boil. Lower heat. Cover and simmer for about 15 minutes, or until potatoes are tender. Stir in clams and half-and-half. Heat soup to simmer. Do not boil. Add salt and pepper to taste.

Serve soup in warm tureen or warm individual soup bowls.
**Makes 4 servings.**

Soups

# Red Clam Chowder

3 tablespoons salad oil or
   margarine
1 medium onion, chopped
2 carrots, chopped
1 stalk celery, chopped
1 green pepper, chopped
2 medium potatoes, peeled and
   diced

1 pound can tomatoes
1/4 teaspoon salt
2 cups water
1 cup clam juice
14–16 ounces canned or fresh
   minced clams
salt and pepper to taste

Combine salad oil, onion, carrots, celery, and green pepper in large saucepan. Sauté for about 3 minutes. Add potatoes, tomatoes, salt, water, and clam juice. Bring to boil. Lower heat. Cover and simmer for about 15 minutes. Add clams. Cover and simmer for about 5 minutes. Add salt and pepper to taste.

Serve soup in warm tureen or warm individual soup bowls.

Makes 6 servings.

# Fishyssoise

**2 cups white fish stock**
2 tablespoons margarine or
   salad oil
1 large onion
3 potatoes, peeled and sliced

1 cup cooked white fish, flaked
2 cups milk or half-and-half
salt and white pepper to taste
snipped chives or dill

Combine margarine and onion in saucepan. Sauté onion for about 2 minutes. Add potatoes and white fish stock. Bring to boil. Lower heat. Cover and simmer for about 20 minutes, or until potatoes are very tender.

Transfer mixture to blender or food processor. Blend until smooth.

Transfer purée to large mixing bowl. Stir in fish and milk.

Chill soup in covered container for about 4 hours. Add salt and white pepper to taste.

Serve soup in chilled bowls. Garnish with snipped chives or dill.

Makes 4 servings.

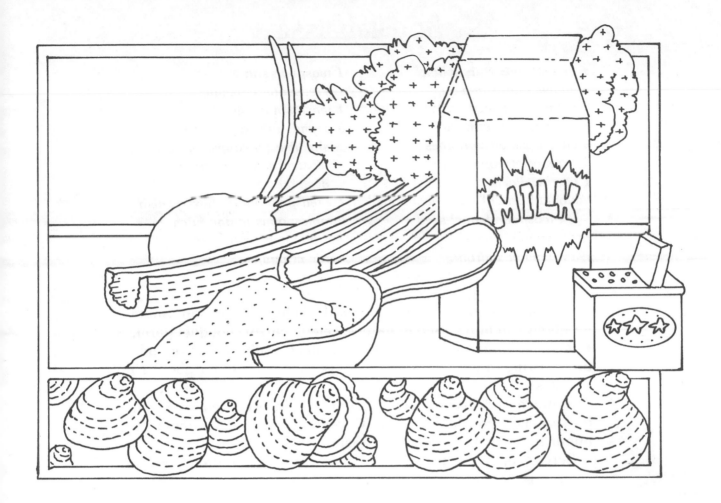

# Chilled Clam and Avocado Soup

**1 cup white fish stock**
*2 medium avocados, peeled,*
*    seeded, and cut into chunks*
*1 cup clam juice*
*1 cup evaporated milk or light*
*    cream*

*2 tablespoons dry sherry*
*14–16 ounces canned or fresh*
*    minced clams*
*salt and pepper to taste*
*chopped parsley*

Combine avocados and clam juice in blender or food processor. Blend until smooth.

Transfer avocado mixture to mixing bowl. Stir in white fish stock, evaporated milk, dry sherry, and minced clams.

Chill soup in covered container for about 4 hours. Add salt and pepper to taste.

Serve soup in chilled bowls. Garnish with chopped parsley.

Makes 4 servings.

Soups

# Bouillabaisse

**6 cups basic fish stock**
3 tablespoons salad oil
2 onions, chopped
1 clove garlic, minced
2 cups crushed tomatoes
1 stalk celery and top, diced
1 carrot, diced
bouquet garni of 1 bay leaf and
   1/4 teaspoon fennel seed
1/2 teaspoon thyme
1/8 teaspoon saffron
2 tablespoons minced parsley

1 teaspoon salt
1/8 teaspoon cayenne
1 teaspoon dulse
3 pounds mixed prepared raw
   shellfish (shrimps, mussels,
   lobster, scallops, clams,
   oysters)
1/2 teaspoon white horseradish
2 tablespoons lemon juice
salt and pepper to taste
garlic croutons

Combine salad oil, onions, and garlic in large saucepan. Sauté for about 2 minutes. Add tomatoes, celery, carrot, bouquet garni, thyme, saffron, parsley, basic fish stock, salt, cayenne, and dulse. Bring to boil. Lower heat. Cover and simmer for about 15 minutes.

Remove and discard bouquet garni. Add prepared shellfish, horseradish, and lemon juice. Cover and simmer for about 10 minutes. Add salt and pepper to taste.

Serve soup in warm tureen with garlic-flavored croutons.

Makes 8 servings.

# Chilled Salmon Bisque

4 tablespoons margarine or
   salad oil
1 small onion, diced
1/2 green pepper, diced
1 cup canned salmon
1 cup milk or half-and-half
1 teaspoon salt

1/4 teaspoon paprika
2 1/2 cups half-and-half or
   evaporated milk
2 tablespoons dry sherry
salt and pepper to taste
1/4 cup minced green pepper

Combine margarine, onion, and green pepper in saucepan. Sauté for about 3 minutes, or until green pepper is tender.

Transfer mixture to blender or food processor. Add salmon and milk. Blend until smooth.

Transfer purée to saucepan. Stir in salt, paprika, and half-and-half. Stir and heat to simmer.

Cool soup at room temperature. Chill in covered container for about 4 hours. Add dry sherry and salt and pepper to taste.

Serve bisque in chilled bowls. Garnish with minced green pepper.

Makes 4 servings.

# Oyster Soup

**3 cups white fish stock**
3 tablespoons salad oil
1 stalk celery, with top, minced
1 small onion, minced
1 clove garlic, finely chopped
  (optional)

2 tablespoons flour
1/4 teaspoon celery salt
8 ounces oysters, canned or
  fresh, shucked
salt and pepper to taste
minced parsley

Combine salad oil, celery, onion, and garlic. Sauté for about 5 minutes. Stir in flour. Stir until blended. Stir in white fish stock and celery salt. Bring to boil. Lower heat. Cover and simmer for about 10 minutes. Add oysters. Simmer for about 3 minutes. Add salt and pepper to taste.

Serve soup in warm tureen or warm individual soup bowls. Garnish with minced parsley.

Makes 4 servings.

Soups

# Oyster Spinach Potage

10-ounce package frozen
  creamed spinach
3 tablespoons margarine
2 tablespoons flour
1/2 teaspoon salt
1/2 teaspoon celery salt
1/8 teaspoon white pepper
1 tablespoon parsley flakes

2 cups milk
8-ounce can whole oysters
  (do not drain)
1 cup light cream or half-and-
  half
1/2 cup dry white wine
salt and pepper to taste
thin lemon slices

Prepare frozen creamed spinach according to package directions. Set aside.

Combine margarine and flour in heavy saucepan. Stir until blended. Add salt, celery salt, and white pepper.

Add creamed spinach to saucepan. Stir in milk. Continue to stir over medium heat until blended. Add oysters and light cream. Heat to simmer. Do not boil. Stir in dry white wine. Add salt and pepper to taste.

Serve soup in warm tureen or warm individual soup bowls. Garnish with thin lemon slices.

Makes 4 servings.

# Shrimp and Mushroom Chowder

2 tablespoons salad oil
1 onion, minced
1 cup clam juice
1 cup water
2 medium potatoes, peeled and diced
1/2 teaspoon salt

3/4 pound small shrimp, peeled and de-veined
1 pound fresh mushrooms, soaked, wiped, and chopped
1 cup light cream or half-and-half
salt and pepper to taste
oyster crackers

Combine salad oil and onion in large saucepan. Sauté onion for about 3 minutes. Add clam juice, water, potatoes, and salt. Bring to boil. Lower heat. Cover and simmer for about 5 minutes.

Transfer about half of potatoes to blender or food processor. Add 1 cup of liquid from saucepan. Blend until smooth.

Return purée to saucepan. Add shrimp and mushrooms. Bring to boil. Lower heat. Cover and simmer for about 5 minutes, or until shrimp are pink. Stir in light cream. Heat to simmer. Do not boil. Add salt and pepper to taste.

Serve chowder in warm tureen or warm individual soup bowls with side dish of oyster crackers.

Makes 4 servings.

# Creamed Mussels and Vegetable Chowder

**3 cups white fish stock**
2 tablespoons salad oil
1 medium onion, chopped
2 medium carrots, diced
2 stalks celery, diced
2 medium potatoes, diced

12-ounce can mussels and liquid or
2 quarts fresh mussels, prepared and cooked, with liquid reserved
2 cups light cream
salt and pepper to taste

Combine salad oil and onion in large saucepan.
Sauté onions for about 3 minutes.

Add white fish stock, carrots, celery, and potatoes. Bring mixture to boil. Lower heat. Cover and simmer for about 15 minutes. Add mussels and liquid. Add light cream. Heat chowder to simmer. Do not boil.

Serve chowder in warm tureen or warm individual soup bowls.
Makes 6 servings.

Soups

# Shellfish Gumbo

3 cups white fish stock
4 tablespoons salad oil
1 1/2 cups okra, fresh or
    defrosted frozen, sliced
1 onion, chopped
1/2 green pepper, chopped
1/4 teaspoon finely chopped
    garlic (optional)
1 tablespoon arrowroot or corn-
    starch
1 cup tomatoes, peeled and
    chopped
1 tablespoon minced parsley
1/2 teaspoon thyme

3/4 teaspoon salt
dash cayenne
1/2 pound raw tiny shrimp,
    fresh or frozen, peeled and
    de-veined
6 ounces lump crabmeat
7–8 ounces minced clams,
    canned or fresh
8 ounces oysters, canned or
    fresh
salt and pepper to taste
1 cup hot cooked rice
minced parsley

Combine salad oil and okra in large saucepan. Sauté okra for about 3 minutes. Stir constantly. Add onion, green pepper, and garlic. Stir and sauté for about 5 minutes.

Combine arrowroot with about 1/4 cup of stock. Stir in white fish stock, arrowroot mixture, tomatoes, parsley, thyme, salt, and cayenne. Bring to boil. Add shrimp. Simmer for about three minutes. Add crabmeat, clams, and oysters. Simmer for about 3 minutes. Add salt and pepper to taste.

Serve soup in warm tureen with portion of rice in each warm individual soup bowl. Garnish with minced parsley.

Makes 6 servings.

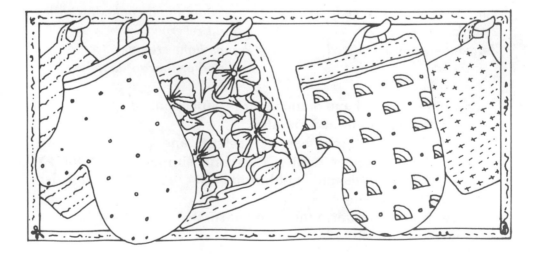

# Fruit Soups

## Chilled Yogurt Fruit Soup

*1-pound can dark sweet
   cherries in heavy syrup*
*3 tablespoons lemon juice*

*1-pound can sliced peaches,
   drained*
*2 cups lemon yogurt*
*1 lemon, sliced very thin*

Combine cherries with syrup and lemon juice in blender or food processor. Blend until smooth. Add peaches. Blend until smooth.
Transfer fruit mixture to mixing bowl. Stir in yogurt.
Chill soup in covered container for about 4 hours.
Serve soup in glass bowls. Garnish with lemon slices.
Makes 6 servings.

Soups

# Iced Orange Strawberry Soup

2 cups frozen strawberries
   (dry pack)
1 cup water
1 cup orange juice

3 tablespoons Grand Marnier
   liqueur
1 cup strawberry yogurt
sprigs fresh mint
fresh strawberry slices

Cut frozen strawberries in half if they are large. Combine strawberries and water in blender or food processor. Blend until smooth. Transfer mixture to large mixing bowl. Whisk in orange juice, liqueur, and yogurt.

Serve soup at once in glass bowls. Garnish with sprigs of mint or fresh strawberry slices.

**Makes 4 servings.**

## ANNIE'S TIPS

Instant homemade soups may be prepared in advance. Keep the soup chilled in an empty quart glass juice bottle. Shake well before serving.

# Iced Strawberry Champagne Soup

2 cups frozen strawberries
(dry pack)
1 bottle chilled champagne

1 cup strawberry yogurt
lemon peel, finely grated

Cut strawberries in half if they are large. Put frozen strawberries in blender or food processor. Blend until smooth.

Divide strawberry slush between four glass bowls.

Let each diner help himself to champagne, stirring it into strawberry slush. Serve strawberry yogurt topped with lemon peel in side dish to be passed as garnish.

Makes 4 servings.

# Cream Fruit Consommé

3 tablespoons margarine
1 small onion, diced
1 apple, cored, peeled, and
diced
1/4 cup apple juice
dash paprika

1/4 teaspoon salt
**3 cups consommé**
1 cup heavy cream
salt and pepper to taste
sliced fresh apples or pears

Combine margarine and onion in saucepan. Sauté onion for about 2 minutes. Add diced apple and sauté for about 3 minutes.

Transfer mixture to blender or food processor. Add apple juice, paprika, and salt. Blend until smooth.

Return purée to saucepan. Add consommé. Heat to boil. Lower heat. Stir in cream. Add salt and pepper to taste. Heat to simmer. Do not boil.

Serve consommé in bouillon cups with side dish of sliced fresh fruit.

Makes 6 servings.

# Rosé Broth with Mandarin Oranges

6 egg whites
1/4 teaspoon cream of tartar
1/2 teaspoon nutmeg
2 cups rosé wine
1 cup orange juice
2 cups water

11-ounce can mandarin orange segments, drained, reserve syrup
3 cinnamon sticks, cracked in half
3 tablespoons lemon juice
1 tablespoon cornstarch

In mixing bowl beat egg whites with cream of tartar and nutmeg. Beat until stiff. Cover mixing bowl and refrigerate.

Combine wine, orange juice, water, reserved syrup, and cinnamon sticks in saucepan. Bring mixture to boil. Lower heat. Simmer for about 4 minutes. Add orange segments to saucepan.

Combine lemon juice with cornstarch. Stir cornstarch mixture into saucepan. Stir constantly until broth thickens. Remove cracked cinnamon sticks and place in each serving bowl. Pour broth over cracked cinnamon sticks. Garnish with stiffly-beaten egg whites.

Makes 6 servings.

# Chilled Raspberry Soup

2 cups raspberries, fresh or frozen dry pack
1 tablespoon honey
1/2 cup dry red wine

1 cup raspberry yogurt
1 cup warm coconut milk
shredded coconut

Combine raspberries, honey, and wine in blender or food processor. Blend until smooth. Strain purée through fine sieve into mixing bowl. Stir in yogurt and coconut milk.

Chill soup in covered container for about 3 hours.

Serve soup in glass bowls. Garnish with shredded coconut.

Makes 4 servings.

ANNIE'S TIPS

Before using prepared chilled coconut milk, heat to blend.

# Rhubarb and Strawberry Soup

4 cups fresh or frozen rhubarb,
  cut into 1-inch pieces
1 cup water
1/4 cup honey
2 cups fresh or frozen strawberries, hulled

1/2  teaspoon nutmeg
1/4 teaspoon salt
1 1/2 cups reserved fruit juice or
  orange juice
ladyfingers

Combine rhubarb and water in saucepan. Bring to boil. Lower heat. Cover and simmer for about 3 minutes.

Combine rhubarb mixture, honey, strawberries, nutmeg, and salt in blender or food processor. Blend until smooth.

Transfer to saucepan. Stir in fruit juice. Heat to simmer.

Serve soup in glass or white bowls with ladyfingers.

**Makes 6 servings.**

Soups

# Chilled Sour Cherry Soup

3 cups water
1 cup granulated sugar
4 cups pitted sour cherries
1 tablespoon cornstarch

1/4 cup water
1/2 cup dry red wine
1/2 cup heavy cream
ground cinnamon

Combine water and sugar in saucepan. Bring mixture to boil. Boil for 3 minutes. Stir and wash down any sugar crystals clinging to sides of saucepan. Lower heat to simmer. Add sour cherries and simmer partially covered for about 35 minutes.

Combine cornstarch with 1/4 cup water. Stir cornstarch mixture into cherry mixture. Simmer for about 5 minutes.

Allow cherry mixture to cool at room temperature. Stir in wine and cream.

Chill soup in covered container for about 6 hours.

Serve soup in glass bowls. Garnish with ground cinnamon.
Makes 4 to 6 servings.

# Cold Fresh Plum Soup

3 cups diced fresh plums
1 quart water
1/2 cup honey
2 tablespoons lemon juice
1/2 inch strip lemon peel

1 stick cinnamon
2 tablespoons cornstarch
1/4 cup cold water
salt and pepper to taste
sour cream

In saucepan combine plums, 1 quart water, honey, lemon juice, lemon peel, and cinnamon stick. Bring mixture to boil. Lower heat and simmer for about 20 minutes, or until plums are very soft. Remove lemon peel and cinnamon stick. Force mixture through food mill. Return mixture to saucepan.

Combine cornstarch and cold water. Stir cornstarch mixture into saucepan. Continue stirring. Bring mixture to boil. Lower heat. Simmer while stirring constantly until soup thickens slightly.

Cool soup at room temperature. Chill soup in covered container for about 6 hours. Add salt and pepper to taste.

Serve soup in glass bowls. Garnish with dollops of sour cream.

**Makes 6 servings.**

# Iced Peach Soup

4 cups peaches, or 20-ounce
   frozen dry pack, cut into
   chunks
1/2 cup water
3 tablespoons honey

1/4 teaspoon cinnamon
1/4 teaspoon curry powder
1/8 teaspoon cloves
1/4 teaspoon salt
2 1/2 cups cold dry white wine
thin slices of orange

Combine peaches, water, honey, cinnamon, curry powder, cloves, and salt in blender or food processor. Blend until smooth.

Transfer peach purée to mixing bowl. Whisk in wine.

Serve soup at once in glass soup bowls. Garnish each serving with slice of orange.

**Makes 6 servings.**

**ANNIE'S TIPS**

Use a brush dipped in cold water to wash down sugar crystals.

# Cold Cherry Wine Soup

1 can dark sweet cherries
  (16 1/2 ounces)
1 cup cherry wine
1 quart water
3 inches stick cinnamon

3 tablespoons small pearl
  tapioca
4 tablespoons honey
1 tablespoon lemon juice
2 egg yolks, beaten
1/2 lemon, sliced thin

Combine canned cherries and wine in blender or food processor. Blend until smooth.

In saucepan, combine cherry and wine mixture with water, stick cinnamon, tapioca, honey, and lemon juice. Bring mixture to boil. Lower heat and simmer for 10 minutes. Remove stick cinnamon.

In mixing bowl add 1 cup of hot liquid from saucepan, very slowly, to egg yolks. Stir egg yolk mixture into saucepan.

Remove saucepan from heat and allow to cool at room temperature. Chill soup in covered container for about 6 hours.

Serve soup in glass bowls. Garnish with lemon slices.
Makes 6 servings.

Soups

# Chilled Honeydew Soup

1 large honeydew melon
6-ounce can frozen lime juice
   concentrate
2 tablespoons ground almonds
3 tablespoons lemon juice

1 teaspoon grated lemon rind
1 1/2 cups cold water
1 cup sour cream
thin slices of lime or fresh mint
   sprigs

Cut melon in half. Remove seeds and membrane. With melon-ball cutter, scoop out flesh from half of melon. Reserve melon balls in covered container in refrigerator.

Remove flesh from second half of melon.

Combine melon, lime juice concentrate, ground almonds, lemon juice, and lemon rind in blender or food processor. Blend until smooth.

Transfer to mixing bowl. Stir in cold water and sour cream. Chill soup in covered container for about 3 hours.

Before serving soup, stir in reserved melon balls. Serve soup in glass bowls. Garnish with lime slices or mint sprigs.

Makes 4 servings.

# Iced Big Blue Soup

1 1/2 cups cold water
3 cups frozen blueberries
   (dry pack)
1 teaspoon lemon juice

1 tablespoon honey
pinch of salt
heavy cream
fresh mint sprigs

Combine water, blueberries, lemon juice, honey, and salt in blender or food processor, in batches if necessary. Blend until smooth.

Pour soup at once into four glass bowls or glass mugs. Carefully pour cream down side of each bowl so thin layer floats on top of soup.

Garnish with fresh mint sprigs. Serve at once.

Makes 4 servings.

Soups

# Chilled Plum Soup

1-pound, 13-ounce can purple
  plums (drain, and reserve
  syrup)
1 cup water
2/3 cup sugar
1 cinnamon stick
1/4 teaspoon white pepper
1/2 teaspoon lemon rind

salt and pepper to taste
1/2 cup dry red wine
1 tablespoon cornstarch
2 tablespoons brandy
1 cup sour cream
1/2 cup heavy cream
ground cinnamon
sour cream

Pit and chop drained plums. Combine plums and reserved syrup in saucepan. Add water, sugar, cinnamon stick, pepper, and lemon rind. Bring mixture to boil. Lower heat and simmer for 5 minutes. Remove cinnamon stick. Add salt and pepper to taste. Combine wine and cornstarch. Stir into saucepan. Continue stirring until mixture thickens. In small mixing bowl, whisk brandy and sour cream with 1 cup of hot soup. Stir mixture into saucepan. Stir in heavy cream. Allow soup to cool at room temperature. Chill soup in covered container for about 6 hours.

Serve soup in glass bowls. Garnish each bowl with dollop of sour cream and sprinkle of ground cinnamon.

Makes 6 servings.

# Tropical Fruit Chowder

**2 cups coconut milk**
1 very ripe banana, mashed
1 cup half-and-half
1/2  cup crushed pineapple,
  drained
1 cup white grapes, cut into
  halves and seeded if
  necessary

2 tablespoons ground almonds
2 tablespoons Cointreau
1/4 teaspoon salt
1 banana, cut into chunks
salt to taste
shredded coconut

Combine mashed banana and coconut milk in saucepan. Heat to boil. Lower heat to simmer. Add half-and-half, pineapple, white grapes, ground almonds, Cointreau, and salt. Heat to simmer. Do not boil. Simmer for about 3 minutes. Add banana chunks. Add salt to taste.

Serve chowder in warm tureen or warm individual soup bowls. Garnish with shredded coconut.

Makes 4 servings.

ANNIE'S TIPS

Before using prepared chilled coconut milk, heat to blend.

# Chilled Tomato Soup

1 cup tomato juice
1 tablespoon salad oil
3 tablespoons lemon juice
1 teaspoon Worcestershire
  sauce
1 slice onion
1 stalk celery, diced

1 tablespoon chopped fresh
  basil
1–2 dashes cayenne pepper
1/2 teaspoon salt
2 cups tomato juice
1 cup yogurt
salt and pepper to taste

Combine 1 cup tomato juice, salad oil, lemon juice, Worcestershire sauce, onion, celery, basil, cayenne pepper, and salt in blender or food processor. Blend until smooth. Transfer mixture to mixing bowl. Stir in 2 cups tomato juice and yogurt.

Chill soup in covered container for about 4 hours. Add salt and pepper to taste.

Serve soup in glass bowls. Garnish with additional chopped basil.

Makes 4 servings.

# Mixed Fruit Soup

12 whole dried apricots, diced
1 1/2 cups dry white wine
4 cups cold water
16 1/2-ounce can pitted cherries, chopped

16-ounce can peaches, chopped
8-ounce can pitted plums, diced
4 tablespoons lemon juice
1 lemon, sliced thin

Soak apricots in wine for 6 hours.

Combine apricot and wine mixture, with cold water in saucepan. Bring mixture to boil. Lower heat and simmer for about 30 minutes. Stir in cherries, peaches, plums, and lemon juice.

Simmer for 5 minutes.

Serve soup in warm tureen or warm individual soup bowls. Garnish with lemon slices.

Makes 6 servings.

# Iced Mixed Melon Soup

4 cups mixed melon balls, or 20
   ounce frozen dry pack
1/2 cup bread crumbs
1/4 cup ground almonds
1 tablespoon salad oil
2 tablespoons lemon juice
2 egg yolks

2 tablespoons chopped fresh
   mint
1 1/2 cups sour milk or buttermilk
salt and pepper to taste
4 sprigs fresh mint

Cut frozen melon balls into chunks. Reserve for later use.

Combine bread crumbs, almonds, salad oil, lemon juice, egg yolks, and chopped mint in blender or food processor. Blend until smooth. Add melon chunks. Blend until smooth.

Transfer mixture to mixing bowl. Whisk in milk. Add salt and pepper to taste.

Serve soup at once in glass bowls. Garnish each serving with sprig of mint.

Makes 4 servings.

ANNIE'S TIPS

When substituting dried herbs for fresh, use half the amount suggested here.

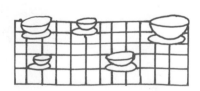

# Iced Anyberry Soup

2 cups frozen berries (dry pack)
4 tablespoons lemon juice
1/3 cup orange juice

2 tablespoons honey
2 cups very cold water
4 sprigs fresh mint

Combine berries, lemon juice, orange juice, and honey in blender or food processor. Blend until smooth.

Transfer mixture to mixing bowl. Stir in very cold water.

Serve soup at once in glass bowls. Garnish each serving with sprig of mint.

**Makes 4 servings.**

## ANNIE'S TIPS

To serve fruit soup as a dessert, add half the suggested amount of water.

# Salads

# First Words
# on Salads

Salads were traditionally served as accompaniments to main courses. But now, it seems they are coming into their own. There's no healthier way to live than by eating lots of fresh fruits and vegetables—but just because salads are so good for you doesn't mean that they have to be dull and uninspired.

It has been said that we eat with our eyes as well as with our taste buds; and so, a variety of shapes and colors will make any salad an all-around enjoyable experience. Always purchase fruits and vegetables that look delicious to begin with. In most cases, you should pass up ones with bruises, blemishes, or broken skins. Ripe, fresh fruit should always be used as soon as possible; unripe fruit should be ripened at room temperature, then stored in the refrigerator. Never wash fruits or vegetables until you're ready to use them, because washing before storage will promote decay. Wrap vegetables in plastic and keep them refrigerated to preserve their crispness until you're ready to use them.

Herbs are the leaves, seeds, and flowers of aromatic plants. Fresh herbs are always preferable, since dried ones may lose their aroma. But if you are using dried herbs, store them in airtight containers kept in a cool place, soak them in water before using them, and use only about half the quantity you would when using fresh herbs.

Spices are the roots, bark, stems, buds, seeds, or fruits of aromatic tropical plants. You should purchase them in small quantities because they tend to quickly lose their flavors. Use both spices and imagination when preparing any of the recipes in this book. Salads should taste as good as they look, so try using a new dressing or adding an extra ingredient for new taste and color.

To enhance your salads' appearance, you can garnish them with almost anything from almonds to zinnias. Serve them on a chilled salad plate or bowl. Glass serving plates complement your salad by allowing all of its colors and textures to be seen. But when you're preparing a recipe that calls for rubbing the bowl with a garlic clove, a wooden bowl is what you need.

**Salads**

# Big Green Salads

## Avocado Spinach Salad

3/4 cup Creamy Bacon Dressing
  (see following recipe)
1 avocado, peeled, seeded,
  sliced in wedges
1 pound raw fresh spinach

1/4 pound fresh raw
  mushrooms, sliced
1 Bermuda onion, sliced thin
2 tablespoons sesame seed

Wash and pat dry spinach leaves. Remove stems and tear spinach leaves into bite-size pieces. Combine spinach with mushrooms, onion, and sesame seed. Arrange spinach mixture in salad bowl with avocado wedges. Top salad with Creamy Bacon Dressing.

  Makes 4 to 6 servings.

### ANNIE'S TIPS

*Use fresh flowers from your garden to enhance the appearance of your salads. Many flowers are edible, but it is best to consider them a decorative garnish.*

Salads

**101**

# Creamy Bacon Dressing

2 tablespoons lemon juice
1/2 cup mayonnaise
1 tablespoon honey

1/8 teaspoon salt
4 slices crisp bacon, crumbled
2 tablespoons onion, finely
   chopped

Add lemon juice to mayonnaise. Stir remaining ingredients.
   Makes 3/4 cup. (Serve immediately on spinach or tossed salad greens.)

# Asparagus and Mushroom Salad

1/2 cup Fines Herbes Vinaigrette
   Dressing (see following recipe)
1/2 pound fresh raw mush-
   rooms, thinly sliced
1 pound asparagus, steamed, cut
   into 1-inch pieces

1 cup yogurt
2 hard-boiled eggs, chopped
1 tablespoon fresh chives,
   chopped

Combine Fines Herbes Vinaigrette Dressing with sliced mushrooms in mixing bowl. Cover and marinate mixture in refrigerator for at least 30 minutes. Steam asparagus until just tender, about 10 minutes.
   Combine yogurt and asparagus. Gently fold asparagus mixture into mushroom mixture. Transfer salad to large serving dish. Garnish with chopped eggs and serve.
   Makes 4 to 6 servings.

# Fines Herbes Vinaigrette

1 teaspoon fresh chives,
   finely chopped
1 tablespoon fresh parsley,
   finely chopped
1 teaspoon prepared French
   mustard

1 garlic clove, crushed
1/2 teaspoon salt
12 tablespoons olive oil
4 tablespoons tarragon vinegar
2 tablespoons lemon juice
1/4 teaspoon black pepper,
   freshly ground

In small mixing bowl, using a wooden spoon, combine chives, parsley, mustard, salt, pepper, and garlic. Gradually stir 3 tablespoons olive oil. Transfer mixture to screw-top jar. Add remaining olive oil, vinegar, and lemon juice. Cover and shake.

Makes 1 cup. (Serve on tossed salad greens or tomato salad.)

# Avocado Gazpacho Salad

*1/4 cup Honey French Dressing
  (see following recipe)*
*4 avocado halves, peeled and
  seeded*
*1/2 cup green pepper, chopped*
*1/2 cup cucumber, chopped*

*1/2 cup tomato, chopped*
*2 tablespoons green onion,
  chopped*
*lettuce leaves*

Combine green pepper, cucumber, tomato, onion, and Honey French Dressing. Mix lightly. Fill avocado halves with vegetable mixture. Place lettuce leaves on 4 individual salad plates. Place avocado halves on plates. Chill well before serving.

Makes 4 servings.

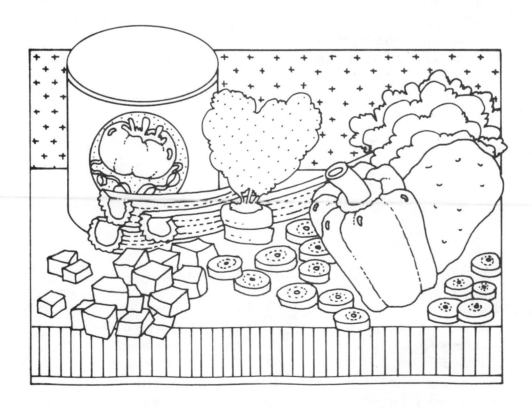

# Honey French Dressing

3/4 cup salad oil
1/4 cup lemon juice
1/2 cup honey
1/2 teaspoon Worcestershire
3/4 teaspoon salt

1/4 teaspoon pepper
1/4 teaspoon paprika
1/4 teaspoon dry mustard
1/2 teaspoon celery seed
small piece lemon rind

Put all ingredients in blender. Blend until smooth.
   Makes 1 1/2 cups. (Serve with tossed salad greens or vegetable salad.)

# Bean Sprout and Cucumber Salad

1/2 cup Ginger Dressing
   (see following recipe)
1/2 pound fresh bean sprouts
2 cucumbers, cut lengthwise in
   1/4-inch slices; cut slices
   into 1/4-inch strips

1 tablespoon salt
1 small onion, sliced thin
1 tablespoon sesame seed
lettuce leaves

Put cucumber in bowl and sprinkle with salt. Let stand for 30 minutes. Put sprouts in colander and pour 1 quart boiling water over them. Refresh sprouts with cold water.
   Drain cucumber and sprouts, and place in clean dry bowl. Add onion and Ginger Dressing to mixture. Toss salad with sesame seed and chill for at least 1 hour. Divide salad into four individual lettuce-lined salad plates.
   Makes 4 servings.

# Ginger Dressing

1 small clove garlic
1 tablespoon fresh ginger,
   chopped

1 strip lemon peel
1/2 cup sesame seed oil
1 cup rice vinegar

Put all ingredients into blender. Blend to creamy stage.
   Makes 1 1/2 cups. (Serve with tossed salad greens.)

# Cheese Spinach Salad

1 cup Ginger Dressing
  (see previous recipe)
1 pound raw fresh spinach
2 hard-boiled eggs,
  finely chopped

1/3 cup finely chopped celery
1/3 cup finely chopped onion
1/2 cup sharp cheese, cubed
1/2 cup mung bean sprouts

Wash and pat dry spinach leaves. Remove stems and tear spinach leaves into bite-size pieces. Combine spinach with eggs, celery, onion, cheese, and sprouts. Toss salad gently with Ginger Dressing. Serve with additional dressing in side dish.
  Makes 4 servings.

# Beet Salad

1 1/2 cups Beet Dressing
  (see following recipe)
1 1/2 pounds fresh beets
1 small clove garlic, halved
1 head lettuce

1/4 cup green onion, sliced
one 7-ounce can tuna, chilled,
  drained, flaked
1/2 cup sliced celery

Cut off all but 1 inch of stem and roots of fresh beets; do not pare. Cook, covered, in boiling salted water about 35 minutes or until tender. Drain, pare, and slice. Chill.
  Just before serving, rub salad bowl with halved garlic. Combine lettuce and onion in salad bowl. Arrange beets, tuna, and celery atop salad greens. Toss salad gently with Beet Dressing. Garnish with additional sliced green onion, if desired.
  Makes 6 to 8 servings.

# Beet Dressing

1 cooked beet, diced
1 sliced onion, minced
1 cup salad oil
2 tablespoons lemon juice

1/4 teaspoon tarragon
1/4 teaspoon dried mustard
1 teaspoon salt
1 small hard-boiled egg, minced

Mix all ingredients together by hand. Chill well before serving.
  Makes about 1 1/2 cups.

### ANNIE'S TIPS

*Prepare dressings well in advance, and chill for at least 1 hour before serving unless directions indicate otherwise.*

Salads

# Broccoli-Tomato Salad

1 cup Cheese and Lemon
   Dressing (see following recipe)
1 bunch broccoli (1/2 pound)

3 medium tomatoes, cut in
   wedges
lettuce leaves

Wash broccoli thoroughly. Remove florets; use stalks another time. Cook florets in boiling salted water for 3 to 4 minutes; or use steamer. Drain well. Cool.

Pour 1 cup Cheese and Lemon Dressing over broccoli. Stir to coat. Chill 2 to 3 hours. Arrange broccoli and tomato wedges on bed of lettuce. Serve with additional dressing in side dish.

Makes 5 to 6 servings.

# Cheese and Lemon Dressing

4 ounces blue cheese, crumbled
1/4 teaspoon grated lemon rind
1/4 cup lemon juice

3/4 cup salad oil
1 teaspoon salt
1 cup dairy sour cream

Blend all ingredients except sour cream in blender or electric mixer. Add sour cream and stir until blended. Chill before serving.
Makes 2 cups. (Serve with seafood or mixed salad greens.)

## ANNIE'S TIPS

*Wash and dry thoroughly all salad greens, fruits, and vegetables just before preparing salad. Never wash fruits or vegetables until ready to use.*

# Cauliflower Salad

1/2 cup Tangy Tomato Dressing
  (see following recipe)
1 small head cauliflower, separated into florets, chopped

6 radishes, chopped fine
1 small onion, chopped fine
lettuce leaves
chopped parsley

Combine cauliflower, onion, and radishes. Mix vegetables with Tangy Tomato Dressing and chill thoroughly. Line a deep salad bowl with lettuce leaves. Fill lined salad bowl with cauliflower salad and garnish with chopped parsley.
  Makes 4 to 6 servings.

# Tangy Tomato Dressing

8-ounce can tomato sauce
2 tablespoons vinegar
1 tablespoon Worcestershire sauce
1 teaspoon sugar
1 teaspoon grated onion

1 teaspoon horseradish
1/2 teaspoon salt
1/4 teaspoon pepper
1 or 2 dashes hot pepper sauce

In screw-top jar, combine all ingredients. Cover and shake.
  Makes 1 cup. (Serve with salad greens or vegetable salad.)

# Celery Slaw

1 1/4 cups Sour Cream Slaw
  Dressing (see following recipe)
1 bunch celery, separated into
  stalks, chopped

3 medium carrots, grated
1 medium onion, diced
lettuce leaves
1/4 cup bean sprouts

Combine celery, carrots, and onion in large mixing bowl. Add Sour Cream Slaw Dressing and combine mixture well. Chill for several hours.
  Serve slaw in lettuce-lined salad bowl. Garnish with sprouts.
  Makes 8 servings.

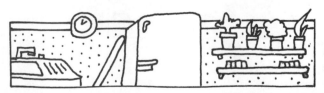

**ANNIE'S TIPS**

*Dressings will store well, refrigerated in tightly-covered jar.*

# Sour Cream Slaw Dressing

1 cup dairy sour cream
1/4 cup vinegar
3 tablespoons sugar

1 1/2 teaspoons salt
1 teaspoon celery seed

Blend all ingredients in blender or electric mixer.
   Makes about 1 1/4 cups.

# Chicken and Ham Salad

1 1/2 cups Creamy Salad
   Dressing (see following recipe)
2 cups cooked chicken, diced
1 1/2 cups cooked ham, cut into
   1/2-inch cubes
2 cups celery, diced
1 cup apple, peeled, cored, diced
1 carrot, cut into thin strips

1 large tomato, diced
1/2 cup seedless green grapes,
   halved
1/2 cup pitted ripe olives, sliced
1 tablespoon finely
   snipped parsley
1/2 teaspoon crushed dried
   rosemary

Combine chicken, ham, celery, apples, tomatoes, grapes, and olives in large bowl. Stir parsley and rosemary into Creamy Salad Dressing. Add dressing to chicken and ham mixture. Toss mixture to coat. Cover bowl and chill. Serve in deep lettuce-lined salad bowl. Garnish with thin carrot strips.
   Makes 8 servings.

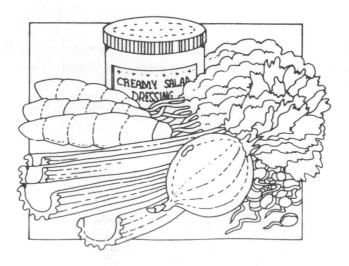

# Creamy Salad Dressing

1/2 cup mayonnaise
1 cup dairy sour cream
1/2 cup parsley sprigs, stems
   removed, minced well
2 tablespoons vinegar

1 teaspoon Worcestershire sauce
1/2 teaspoon salt
1 onion, finely chopped
1 cup pitted ripe olives,
   chopped, drained

Blend all ingredients except onion and olives in blender or electric mixer. Add onions and olives.
   Makes about 1 1/2 cups.(Serve on vegetable or potato salad.)

# Buz's Mixed Seafood Salad

1 cup Dill Sour Cream Dressing
   (see following recipe)
2 cups cooked mixed shellfish
   (crabmeat, lobster, shrimp),
   peeled and cleaned
1 small head iceberg lettuce,
   torn in bite-size pieces
1 cup red cabbage, shredded

1 cup grated carrot
1/2 cup diced green pepper
1 medium cucumber, pared and
   sliced
1/2 pound fresh raw
   mushrooms, sliced
1 teaspoon celery seed

Prepare shellfish and combine in bowl. Set aside. In large salad bowl combine lettuce, cabbage, carrots, green peppers, cucumbers, and mushrooms. Add prepared shellfish to salad mixture. Chill for at least 1 hour.
   Pour Dill Sour Cream Dressing over salad. Add celery seed and toss.
   Makes 6 to 8 servings.

# Dill Sour Cream Dressing

1 1/2 teaspoons lemon juice
1/2 cup dairy sour cream
1 tablespoon mayonnaise
1/8 teaspoon dry mustard

dash cayenne
dash salt
2 sprigs fresh dill

Blend all ingredients in blender or electric mixer. Chill for 2 hours before serving.
   Makes 1/2 cup. (Serve with seafood salad.)

Salads

# Crab Salad

*1/2 cup Dill Sour Cream Dressing*
  *(p.109)*
*1 small head lettuce, shredded*
*1 pound backfin crabmeat*
*4 scallions, finely chopped*
*1/4 pound raw fresh*
  *mushrooms, sliced*

*3 hard-boiled eggs,*
  *cut into wedges*
*3 medium ripe tomatoes,*
  *cut into wedges*
*1/2 cup black pitted olives*

Combine crabmeat with scallions and mushrooms. Add 1/2 cup Dill Sour Cream Dressing. Arrange crabmeat mixture in mound on shredded lettuce. Arrange eggs, tomatoes, and olives around the salad. Serve with additional dressing in side dish.
  Makes 4 servings.

# Cucumber and Shrimp Salad

*1/2 cup Dill Sour Cream Dressing*
  *(p.109)*
*3 large cucumbers, pared*
*1 tablespoon salt*

*1 cup tiny shrimp, cooked,*
  *peeled, and cleaned*
*lettuce leaves*

Prepare shrimp. Refrigerate in covered bowl. Halve cucumbers lengthwise and slice very thin. Put cucumbers in bowl and sprinkle with salt. Let stand for 30 minutes.
  Drain cucumbers and squeeze out excess moisture. Put

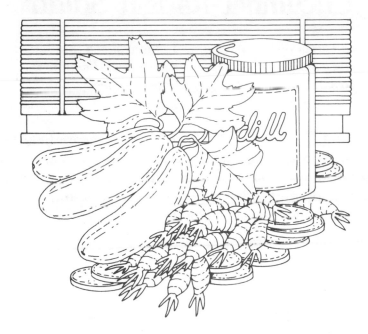

cucumbers in clean dry bowl. Add Dill Sour Cream Dressing. Cover bowl and chill for at least 2 hours. Stir shrimp into cucumber mixture just before serving. Serve in lettuce-lined salad bowl.
Makes 4 servings.

# Tomatoes Stuffed with Shrimp Salad

1/2 cup Dill Sour Cream Dressing
  (p.109)
6 large firm tomatoes
3/4 teaspoon salt
1 medium cucumber, peeled,
  seeded, and chopped

1 pound small shrimps, peeled
  and chopped
lettuce leaves
6 fresh dill sprigs

Put cucumbers in bowl and sprinkle with 3/4 teaspoon salt. Let stand for 30 minutes. Drain. Cut tops off tomatoes. Use grapefruit knife to remove seeds and pulp. Chop pulp and drain in sieve. Sprinkle insides of each tomato with salt and invert on paper towel to drain for at least 30 minutes.

Reserve 6 shrimps from pound for garnish. Chop remaining shrimp coarsely and place in mixing bowl. Add drained cucumbers and tomato pulp to shrimps. Add Dill Sour Cream Dressing and mix well. Chill.

Fill tomato shells with shrimp mixture. Place each stuffed tomato on lettuce-lined salad plate. Garnish top of each stuffed tomato with a whole shrimp and sprig of dill.
Makes 6 servings.

Salads

# Cucumber-Radish Salad

1 cup Lemon-Cucumber
  Dressing (see following recipe)
1 tablespoon salt
3 medium cucumbers, pared

1 onion, sliced thin
6 radishes, sliced thin
lettuce leaves
2 tablespoons chopped walnuts

Halve cucumbers lengthwise and slice. Put cucumbers in bowl and sprinkle with salt. Let stand for 30 minutes. Drain cucumbers and squeeze out excess moisture. Put cucumbers in clean dry bowl. Add onion and radishes. Add Lemon-Cucumber Dressing and mix well. Chill for at least 3 hours.

Transfer mixture to lettuce-lined salad bowl and garnish with walnuts.

Makes 4 servings.

# Lemon-Cucumber Dressing

1 cup mayonnaise
1 cup cucumber, seeded and
  finely chopped
2 tablespoons lemon juice

1 tablespoon onion, minced
2 tablespoons grated lemon peel
1 teaspoon salt
1 cup plain yogurt

Combine all ingredients, except yogurt. Fold in yogurt. Chill before serving.

Makes 2 1/2 cups. (Serve over greens.)

# Gazpacho Salad

1 recipe Avocado Dressing
  (see following recipe)
4 medium tomatoes, sliced thin
1 cucumber, sliced thin
1 small Spanish onion, sliced thin
4 radishes, sliced thin

1/2 cup sprouts
1/4 pound fresh raw
  mushrooms, sliced thin
2 cups red cabbage, shredded
2 tablespoons minced parsley
1/2 cup croutons

In a glass bowl arrange layers of tomatoes, cucumber, onion, radishes, mushrooms, and cabbage. Pour Avocado Dressing over vegetables. Cover bowl and chill for 4 hours.

Just before serving, garnish salad with sprouts, parsley, and croutons.

Makes 4 servings.

Salads

# Avocado Dressing

1 ripe avocado, peeled and seeded
4 tablespoons mayonnaise
2 tablespoons lemon juice
1/2 teaspoon salt

1/2 teaspoon horseradish
1/8 teaspoon cayenne
1 clove garlic (optional)

Mash avocado and lemon juice with fork until smooth. Mix in mayonnaise, horseradish, and cayenne. Squeeze garlic through press. Mix all ingredients well. Add salt to taste.

Makes about 1/2 cup. (Serve with tossed salad greens or tomato and lettuce.)

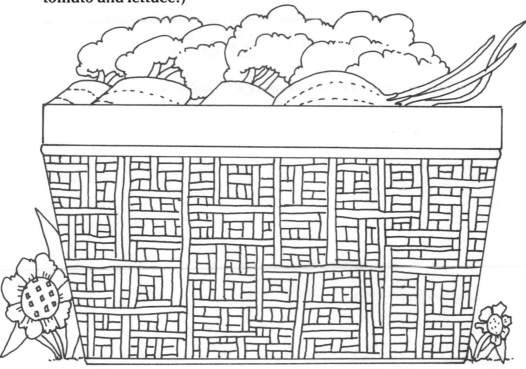

# Green Salad with Hard-Boiled Egg

1 cup Herbed Sour Cream
  Dressing (see following recipe)
1 head Boston lettuce, torn
  in bite-size pieces

3 hard-boiled eggs, sliced
1/4 cup scallion, minced
1 hard-boiled egg, chopped
paprika

Combine Boston lettuce, sliced eggs, and scallions in salad bowl. Add Herbed Sour Cream Dressing and toss salad. Garnish with chopped egg and sprinkle salad with paprika.

Makes 4 servings.

## ANNIE'S TIPS

*Yield of avocado dressing will vary with size of avocado.*

# Herbed Sour Cream Dressing

| | |
|---|---|
| 1 cup dairy sour cream | 1/2 teaspoon salt |
| 2 tablespoons red wine vinegar | 1/2 teaspoon celery seed |
| 1 teaspoon sugar | 1/4 teaspoon thyme |

Mix all ingredients until well blended. Chill before serving.
Makes about 1 cup.

# Marinated Zucchini with Tomato Salad

| | |
|---|---|
| 1 cup Yogurt Dressing Supreme (see following recipe) | 2 medium tomatoes, sliced |
| lettuce leaves | 1 pound zucchini, thinly sliced (2 cups) |

Steam zucchini until tender-crisp, about 2 to 3 minutes. Drain well. Add Yogurt Dressing Supreme to zucchini. Toss to coat. Chill for about 2 to 3 hours.

Arrange tomato slices on lettuce leaves on platter. Top platter with marinated zucchini.

Makes 4 to 5 servings.

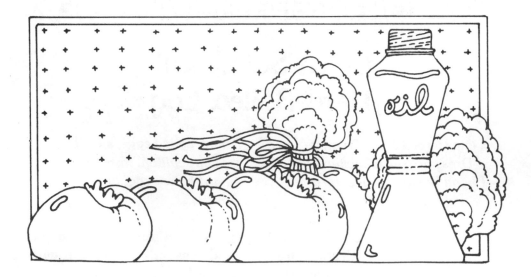

**Salads**

**ANNIE'S TIPS**

*It has been said by many that we eat with our eyes.*

# Yogurt Dressing Supreme

1/2 cup yogurt

1/4 cup lemon juice

1/2 cup creamed cottage
cheese

1 teaspoon salt

1/2 teaspoon paprika

1/2 green pepper, seeded and
minced

Blend all ingredients, except green pepper, in blender or electric mixer. Blend until smooth. Add green pepper and mix well by hand. Chill well before serving.

Makes 1 cup. (Serve with vegetable salad or with seafood.)

# Japanese Salad

1/4 cup Oriental Dressing
(see following recipe)

2 small carrots, cut in strips

1 small zucchini, cut in strips

1 cucumber, cut in strips

1/2 cup bean sprouts

1/2 cup celery, diced

1/2 cup fresh raw mushrooms,
sliced

1/2 cup watercress

lettuce leaves

Combine all vegetables except lettuce in bowl. Add Oriental Dressing to vegetables and toss well. Serve in lettuce-lined salad bowl.

Makes 4 servings.

# Oriental Dressing

1 tablespoon lemon juice

1 teaspoon grated lemon peel

1/2 teaspoon soy sauce

1/2 teaspoon prepared mustard

1 teaspoon rice vinegar

1 tablespoon salad oil

Combine all ingredients into a blender and blend. Chill before serving.

Makes 1/4 cup. (Serve with fresh vegetable salad.)

**ANNIE'S TIPS**

*Try substituting the suggested dressing with your own favorite dressing.*

Salads

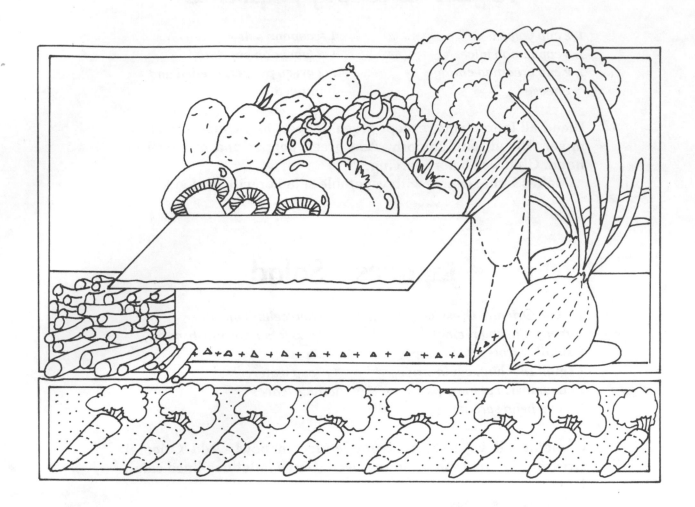

# Mixed Salad

1 scant cup French Mustard
  Dressing (see following recipe)
1 medium cucumber, pared
1 avocado, peeled, pitted,
  and sliced
2 large bananas, sliced
lettuce leaves

1 large green pepper, seeded, cut
  in thin strips
1 mild red pepper, seeded, cut in
  thin strips
1/2 small onion, very thinly
  sliced and separated into rings

Halve cucumber lengthwise; remove seeds and slice crosswise.
Combine cucumber with avocado, bananas, peppers, and onion
in salad bowl. Pour French Mustard Dressing over mixture. Cover
salad bowl and marinate in refrigerator for about 2 hours.
   Toss mixture gently and serve in lettuce-lined bowl.
   Makes 6 servings.

Salads

116

# French Mustard Dressing

2 full teaspoons Grey Poupon®
   mustard
1/2 teaspoon salt

1/3 cup red wine vinegar, scant
1/3 cup corn oil, scant
1/4 teaspoon black pepper

In screw-top jar combine all ingredients. Cover and shake well.
   Makes about 3/4 cup. (Serve with tomatoes marinated in dressing.)

# Marinated Avocado-Mushroom Salad

1/2 cup White Wine Dressing
   (see following recipe)
1 medium avocado, seeded,
   peeled, and sliced

lettuce leaves
1 cup fresh raw mushrooms,
   sliced
2 medium onions, sliced thin

Combine avocado and mushrooms in bowl. Separate onions into rings and add to avocado mixture. Pour White Wine Dressing over vegetables. Cover bowl and marinate in refrigerator for about 3 hours.
   Drain avocado mixture. Spoon mixture into lettuce-lined salad plate.
   Makes 4 servings.

# White Wine Dressing

1/2 cup light salad oil
1/2 cup dry white wine
2 tablespoons vinegar

1/2 teaspoon sugar
1/2 teaspoon salt
1/2 teaspoon dried basil,
   crushed

Combine all ingredients in screw-top jar. Cover and shake well. Chill before serving.
   Makes about 1 cup. (Serve with mixed vegetable salad or use as marinade for fresh vegetables.)

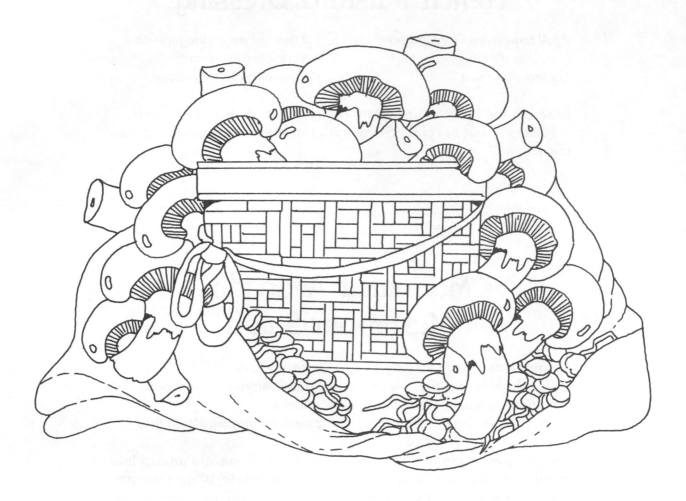

# Bean Sprout and Mushroom Salad

*1/2 cup White Wine Dressing*
*(see previous recipe)*
*1 medium onion, sliced thin*
*2 tablespoons butter*

*1/2 pound fresh raw*
*mushrooms, sliced*
*1 pound fresh bean sprouts*
*1 tablespoon sesame seed*
*lettuce leaves*

In a skillet sauté sliced onion in butter for 1 minute. Add mushrooms to skillet and sauté mixture until mushrooms are just wilted. Transfer mixture to bowl.

Put sprouts in colander and pour 1 quart boiling water over them. Drain sprouts and add to bowl containing mushroom mixture. Pour White Wine Dressing over vegetables in bowl and add sesame seed. Toss salad well and chill for at least 1 hour. Divide mixture into 4 individual lettuce-lined salad plates.

Makes 4 servings.

**Salads**

# Mushroom and Bacon Salad

1 cup White Wine Dressing (p.117)
1/4 teaspoon freshly ground
   black pepper
1 pound fresh raw mushrooms,
   sliced thin
6 strips bacon, cooked crisp,
   drained, crumbled

2 celery stalks, trimmed,
   finely chopped
1 tablespoon fresh parsley,
   chopped
1 tablespoon fresh chives,
   chopped
lettuce leaves

Combine White Wine Dressing, black pepper, and mushrooms in mixing bowl. Cover bowl and chill for about 30 minutes. Arrange lettuce leaves on individual salad plates.

Use slotted spoon to transfer mushrooms onto lettuce leaves. Reserve dressing to serve over salad. Add celery, bacon, parsley, and chives to each salad plate. Serve immediately with reserved dressing in sauce dish.

Makes 6 servings.

# Sesame Lettuce Salad

1 1/2 cups French-Style Blue
   Cheese Dressing
   (see following recipe)
2 tablespoons sesame seed
1 small head lettuce

1/2 cup green pepper, chopped
2 green onions, sliced
one 11-ounce can mandarin
   orange sections, drained
1/2 medium cucumber, sliced

In skillet, toast sesame seed till lightly browned. Add sesame seed to French-Style Blue Cheese Dressing. Combine lettuce, green pepper, and onions. Arrange lettuce mixture, orange sections, and cucumber in salad bowl. Pour salad dressing atop, toss lightly, and serve.

Makes 4 to 6 servings.

# French-Style Blue Cheese Dressing

1 cup salad oil
3 tablespoons lemon juice
1 teaspoon sugar
1/2 teaspoon salt

4 ounces blue cheese, crumbled
2 teaspoons paprika
1 slice onion, minced

Mix all ingredients with electric mixer. Chill well before serving.
   Makes about 1 1/2 cups. (Serve with salad greens.)

**Salads**

119

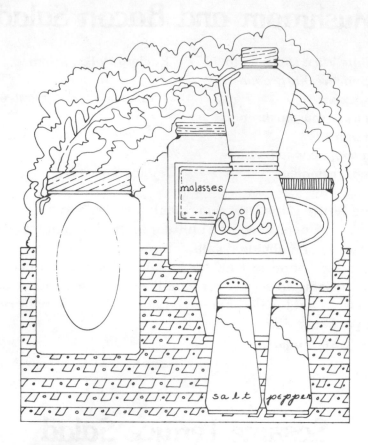

# Special Tossed Romaine

1 cup Parmesan Dressing Rosé
(see following recipe)

6 strips bacon, cooked crisp,
drained, crumbled

2 heads romaine, torn in
bite-size pieces

2 cups cherry tomatoes, halved

1 cup Swiss cheese,
coarsely grated

2/3 cup slivered almonds,
toasted

1/3 cup Parmesan cheese,
grated

1 cup croutons

Combine bacon, romaine, tomatoes, Swiss cheese, almonds, and
Parmesan cheese in large salad bowl. Toss salad with Parmesan
Dressing Rosé. Add salt and pepper to taste. Garnish with
croutons.

Makes 8 servings.

# Parmesan Dressing Rosé

1 egg

3/4 cup salad oil

1/2 cup rosé wine

3 tablespoons Parmesan cheese,
grated

3 tablespoons wine vinegar

1/4 teaspoon seasoned salt

1/4 teaspoon paprika

1/2 clove garlic

Put all ingredients in blender. Blend until garlic is liquefied.

Makes 1 1/2 cups. (Serve with vegetables or tossed salad greens.)

# Tomato Salad Rosé

*1 1/2 cups Parmesan Dressing
    Rosé (see previous recipe)*
*4 large tomatoes, peeled and
    thinly sliced*

*1/2 cup celery, finely chopped*
*1 small onion, sliced thin*
*lettuce leaves*

Place tomatoes, celery, and onion in shallow dish or deep bowl. Pour Parmesan Dressing Rosé over tomato mixture. Cover and chill for several hours.

Lift tomato mixture from dressing and spread onto lettuce leaves. Spoon some dressing over tomatoes. Serve with additional dressing in side dish.

Makes 4 to 6 servings.

**Salads**

# Special Green Salad

2 1/2 cups Tomato Honey
   Dressing (see following recipe)
1 small head iceberg lettuce
1/2 pound fresh spinach
1 cup curly escarole

1 medium cucumber, sliced thin
1/2 pound raw fresh mushrooms
1 Bermuda onion, sliced
1/2 cup alfalfa or mung-bean
   sprouts

Wash lettuce, spinach, and escarole. Pat dry and tear into bite-size pieces. Place greens in salad bowl. Add cucumber, mushrooms, onion, and sprouts to salad greens. Toss salad gently with 1 cup Tomato Honey Dressing. Serve with additional dressing in a side dish.

   Makes 4 to 6 servings.

# Tomato Honey Dressing

1 cup salad oil
1/2 cup catsup
1/3 cup vinegar
1/3 cup honey

1 teaspoon salt
1 teaspoon paprika
1 thin slice onion
1/4 clove garlic

Put all ingredients in blender. Blend until onion slice and garlic are liquefied. Chill well before serving.

   Makes 2 1/2 cups. (Serve with tossed salad greens or vegetable salad.)

# Tomato-Beef Salad

1 2/3 cups Horseradish Dressing
   (see following recipe)
3 medium tomatoes, sliced
lettuce leaves

1 pound sliced cold roast beef
2 small green onions,
   sliced in rings

Line platter with lettuce. Arrange slices of roast beef and tomato on top of lettuce. Pour 2/3 cup Horseradish Dressing over beef and tomatoes. Arrange onion slices on platter. Serve with additional dressing in side dish.

   Makes 3 to 4 servings.

### ANNIE'S TIPS

*Save used mayonnaise jars for dressing storage. Wide-mouth jars are most convenient for this purpose.*

# Horseradish Dressing

1 cup mayonnaise
1/2 cup buttermilk
2 tablespoons green onion,
   finely chopped

1 1/2 tablespoons horseradish
1/2 teaspoon salt
1/8 teaspoon white pepper

Combine all ingredients. Chill before serving.
   Makes 1 2/3 cups. (Serve with vegetable salad with beef.)

# Sweet Pepper Salad

1 cup Wine Dressing
   (see following recipe)
4 green peppers
4 red peppers

16 pitted black olives
8 ounces cream cheese,
   cut into cubes

Wash peppers and cut into halves. Remove seeds and white pith.
Cut each half into quarters. Steam peppers for 3 minutes.
Remove from steamer and let cool on paper towel. Combine peppers
with Wine Dressing in mixing bowl. Cover and marinate in
refrigerator for about 24 hours.
   To serve, place marinated peppers in shallow bowl. Arrange
olives and cream cheese atop peppers. Spoon a little marinade
over salad.
   Makes 4 to 6 servings.

# Wine Dressing

6 tablespoons white wine vinegar
3 tablespoons medium dry sherry
1 tablespoon Worcestershire sauce
6 tablespoons olive oil
1/2 teaspoon seasoned salt

1/2 teaspoon salt
1/4 teaspoon pepper
2 tablespoons sugar
1 teaspoon paprika

Combine all ingredients in screw-top jar. Cover and shake until
well blended. Chill before serving.
   Makes 1 cup. (Serve on mixed vegetable salad.)

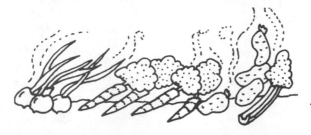

**ANNIE'S TIPS**

*Wrap vegetables in plastic
wrap and keep re-
frigerated until ready to
use.*

Salads

# Tuna Salad
# in Pepper Cups

3/4 cup Creamy Bacon Dressing (p.102)
5 medium green peppers, halved
   lengthwise, seeded
2 medium carrots, grated
2 stalks celery, chopped
lettuce leaves

2 tablespoons chopped onion
one 7-ounce can tuna,
   drained and flaked
1 medium firm tomato, sliced
   very thin
snipped parsley

Substitute honey with 1 tablespoon prepared mustard when preparing Creamy Bacon Dressing. Steam peppers for 5 minutes. Drain and chill.

Combine carrots, celery, onion, and tuna in mixing bowl. Pour Creamy Bacon Dressing over tuna mixture and toss lightly. Chill. Sprinkle inside of peppers with salt. Fill peppers with tuna mixture.

Serve stuffed peppers on lettuce-lined plates. Garnish top of each pepper with sliced tomato and parsley.

Makes 5 servings.

# Vegetable Salad Plate
# with Dip

2 cups Two-Cheese Dressing
   (see following recipe)
1 small bunch celery, separated
   into stalks
1/2 pound string beans,
   snap ends
1 green pepper, seeded and sliced
1 head cauliflower, separated
   into florets

2 small cucumbers, peeled, cut
   into quarters lengthwise
1 bunch radishes, sliced thick
1/2 pound fresh raw
   mushrooms, sliced thick
1 pint cherry tomatoes
olives stuffed with pimento
parsley

Place saucedish in center of large round platter. Arrange prepared vegetables on platter to look like pie wedges. Fill saucedish with Two-Cheese Dressing. Garnish salad plate with olives and parsley.

Serve as hors d'oeuvre.

ANNIE'S TIPS

*Keep vegetables cold and crisp unless recipe indicates otherwise.*

# Two-Cheese Dressing

3/4 cup milk
one 8-ounce package cream
   cheese, cubed
one 4-ounce package blue cheese

1/2 teaspoon tarragon
1 teaspoon salt
1/4 teaspoon pepper
1/4 clove garlic

Put all ingredients in blender. Blend until smooth and garlic is liquefied. Chill well before serving.

   Makes about 2 cups. (Serve with vegetable salad.)


# Tomatoes Stuffed with Beets

1 1/2 cups Tarragon Sour
   Cream Dressing (see following recipe)
3 1/2 cups cooked or canned
   beets, drained and minced
4 large firm tomatoes

salt
lettuce leaves
fresh tarragon, minced
snipped parsley

Cut tops off tomatoes. Use grapefruit knife to remove seeds and pulp. Sprinkle insides of each tomato with salt, and invert on paper towel to drain for at least 30 minutes.

   In bowl combine beets with Tarragon Sour Cream Dressing. Fill tomato shells with beet mixture. Chill stuffed tomatoes for at least 1 hour.

   Serve each tomato on lettuce-lined salad plate. Garnish with minced fresh tarragon and snipped parsley.

   Makes 4 servings.

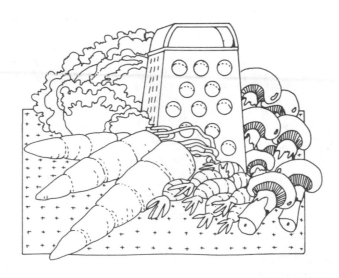

# Tarragon Sour Cream Dressing

1 1/2 teaspoons tarragon,
  crumbled
4 teaspoons white wine vinegar
1 1/2 cups sour cream

1 teaspoon sugar
3/4 teaspoon salt
1/4 teaspoon white pepper

Soak tarragon in vinegar for at least 1 hour. Add sugar, sour cream, salt, and white pepper to vinegar. Mix well. Chill before serving.

Makes about 1 1/2 cups. (Serve with fresh vegetable salad or seafood salad.)

# Vegetable-Shrimp Salad

3/4 cup Tarragon Sour Cream
  Dressing (see previous recipe)
1 pound cooked shrimp, peeled
  and cleaned
3 large carrots, grated

1 1/2 cups small green beans,
  snap ends, cut lengthwise
1/2 pound fresh raw
  mushrooms, sliced thin
lettuce leaves

Prepare shrimp. Refrigerate in covered bowl. Combine carrots, green beans, and mushrooms in bowl. Add shrimp and Tarragon Sour Cream Dressing. Toss salad lightly. Serve in lettuce-lined salad bowl.

Makes 4 servings.

**Salads**

ANNIE'S TIPS

*Serve salads in chilled bowl or salad plate.*

# Fruit Salads

## Tossed Fruit Salad

2 cups Lemon Dressing
   (see following recipe)
3 pears, peeled, cored, sliced
2 medium bananas, sliced
1 medium orange, peeled,
   sectioned, seeded

1 cup pineapple, chopped
1/2 cup walnuts, chopped
cinnamon
lettuce leaves

Combine fruits and walnuts in deep bowl. Toss fruits and walnuts with Lemon Dressing. Chill for several hours. Line serving bowl with lettuce leaves and fill with fruit salad. Sprinkle with cinnamon.

   Makes 6 servings.

Salads

127

# Lemon Dressing

1 cup mayonnaise
1 tablespoon grated lemon peel

2 teaspoons celery seed
1 cup lemon yogurt

Combine lemon peel and celery seed with mayonnaise. Fold yogurt into mayonnaise mixture. Chill before serving.
  Makes 2 cups. (Serve on vegetable salad or fruit salad.)

# Apple-Raisin Slaw

1 cup Lemon Dressing
  (see previous recipe)
1 cup golden raisins
1 cup rosé wine

1 tablespoon lemon juice
3 apples, cored and diced
4 cups cabbage, shredded

Combine raisins and wine. Cover and let stand for several hours. Sprinkle lemon juice over apples. Add raisin-and-wine mixture to apples. Combine mixture with cabbage. Toss with Lemon Dressing. Chill before serving.
  Make 6 servings.

# Poached Naval Orange Salad

6 naval oranges, peeled, and
  sectioned
1 orange rind, cut very fine
2/3 cup orange juice

2/3 cup water
2/3 cup honey
lettuce leaves
1 cup yogurt

After peeling oranges remove all white membrane. Place orange rind in saucepan with water, orange juice, and honey. Simmer for 10 minutes, stirring frequently. Remove oranges from sauce and chill.
  Strain sauce. Blend 2 tablespoons of sauce with yogurt. Line 6 salad plates with lettuce leaves. Arrange chilled oranges on salad plates. Spoon yogurt mixture over oranges.
  Makes 6 servings.

# Bananas and Pears with Port

3 pears, peeled, cored, sliced
2 bananas, sliced
1/4 cup golden raisins
1/4 cup sliced almonds

1/2 cup sweet Port wine
1/4 cup orange juice
2 tablespoons lemon juice
lettuce leaves

Combine pears, bananas, raisins, and almonds in bowl. Add Port, orange juice, and lemon juice. Toss mixture lightly. Cover and chill for at least 3 hours. Serve in lettuce-lined salad cups.
   Makes 4 servings.

# Banana Split Salad

1 cup Mocha Dressing
   (see following recipe)
endive
4 bananas

1 pint strawberries
1/2 cup coconut
1 cup blueberries

Line 4 banana-split dishes with endive. Peel bananas and slice in half lengthwise. Place sliced banana atop each lined dish. Reserve four large strawberries for garnish. Hull and slice remaining strawberries. Combine sliced strawberries, blueberries, and coconut. Divide mixture between the four dishes. Spoon about 1/4 cup Mocha Dressing atop each salad. Garnish each dish with whole strawberry.
   Makes 4 servings.

# Mocha Dressing

1 cup coffee yogurt
1 tablespoon cocoa, sifted

1 tablespoon honey
1/4 teaspoon cinnamon

Combine cocoa, honey, and cinnamon with yogurt in small bowl. Stir to blend. Chill before serving.
   Makes 1 cup. (Serve on fruit salad.)

Salads

# Beet Fruit Salad

3 tablespoons red wine vinegar
1 teaspoon tarragon, crumbled
1/2 cup sugar
3 beets, cooked, peeled,
   chopped, salted
lettuce leaves

3 naval oranges,
   peeled, sectioned
3 bananas, sliced
3 tart apples, cored, sliced
1/3 cup walnuts, chopped

Combine tarragon, sugar, and vinegar in bowl. Add beets and onion. Add oranges, bananas, and apples. Cover bowl and chill for at least 2 hours. Serve on lettuce-lined chilled platter. Garnish with walnuts.

    Makes 8 servings.

# Cheese and Fruit Salad

1/2 pint cottage cheese
1/2 pound Danish blue cheese
1/2 cup sour cream
lettuce leaves
apple wedges

fresh pears, sliced
white seedless grapes
strawberries
mint leaves

Beat cheese and sour cream until well blended. Arrange cheese mixture in center of plate lined with lettuce leaves. Chill. Arrange prepared fresh fruit around cheese. Decorate top of cheese with mint leaves.

    Makes 8 to 10 servings.

# Citrus Salad

1 1/2 cups Citrus Dressing
   (see following recipe)
6 oranges, peeled, seeded,
   sectioned
lettuce leaves

2 avocados, peeled, seeded,
   sliced
3 grapefruits, peeled, seeded,
   sectioned

Line individual salad plates with lettuce leaves. Arrange orange sections, grapefruit sections, and avocado slices on each plate. Spoon Citrus Dressing over each salad. Serve with additional dressing on table.

    Makes 6 servings.

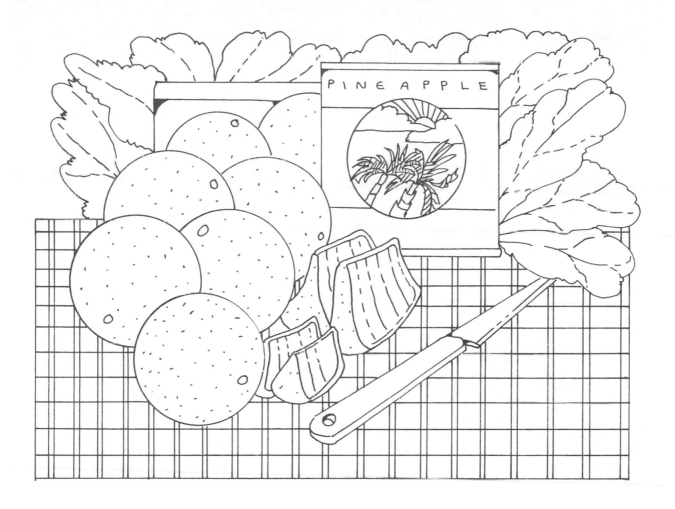

# Citrus Dressing

1/4 cup sugar  
1 teaspoon salt  
1 teaspoon paprika

1 teaspoon dry mustard  
1/3 cup lime juice  
2/3 cup salad oil

**Blend all ingredients in electric blender for 15 seconds on high speed.**

**Makes 1 1/2 cups. (Serve on citrus salad or avocado salad.)**

### ANNIE'S TIPS

*Remove the white membrane, called pith, from citrus fruit after peeling. The pith has a bitter taste.*

**Salads**

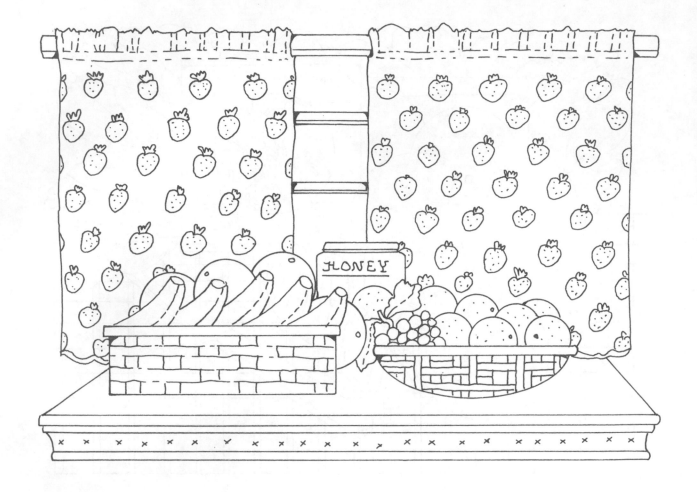

# Fruit Salad Platter

1 recipe Fresh Fruit Dressing
   (see following recipe)
3 grapefruits
6 oranges, peeled and sectioned
1 can pineapple spears, drained

3 tangerines
2 cups cream-style cottage
   cheese
romaine leaves

Line platter with romaine. Put cottage cheese in small glass bowl
and place on platter. Arrange fruits atop romaine. Serve Fresh
Fruit Dressing in separate dish and spoon over fruit salad platter.
   Makes 8 servings.

ANNIE'S TIPS

*Do not wash fruit until
ready to use. Washing
fruit before use will promote decay.*

# Fresh Fruit Dressing

4 egg yolks  
1/4 cup sugar  
pinch of salt  

1/4 cup Marsala wine  
pinch of ground nutmeg  

In a saucepan beat yolks, sugar, and salt until light and lemon-colored. Place saucepan over boiling water and continue beating, adding wine and nutmeg until thick and mixture mounds. Chill before serving.

Makes about 3/4 cup. (Serve with fresh fruit salad.)

# Fruit Salad with Shrimp

1/2 cup Dill Sour Cream Dressing (p.109)  
1 1/2 pounds cooked tiny shrimp  
2 tablespoons lemon juice  
2 tablespoons lime juice  
4 ounces shredded coconut  
2 thinly sliced bananas  

4-ounce can chunky pineapple, drained  
4 medium tomatoes, cut in quarters, seeded, diced  
1 red pepper, seeded, chopped  
1 green pepper, seeded, chopped  

Combine shrimps in mixing bowl with lemon juice and lime juice. Toss mixture, cover, and refrigerate. In large mixing bowl combine coconut, bananas, pineapple, tomatoes, red pepper, and green pepper. Toss mixture with 1/2 cup Dill Sour Cream Dressing. Add shrimps and toss again. Cover bowl and chill for at least 1 hour before serving.

Makes 6 servings.

# Ginger Summer Salad

1/2 cup blueberries  
1 cup honeydew balls  
1 cup cantaloupe balls  
1 cup watermelon balls  
1 pint strawberries, hulled, halved if large  

2 small bananas, sliced  
1 cup seedless grapes  
1/4 cup honey  
1/4 cup lime juice  
1/4 teaspoon ginger  

Combine fruits in large bowl. Mix honey, lime juice, and ginger. Pour mixture over fruit. Toss fruit salad gently and chill for several hours before serving.

Makes 6 to 8 servings.

Salads

# Holiday Fruit Salad

2 1/2 cups Orange-Honey Fruit
   Dressing (see following recipe)
1 cup raw cranberries, chopped
2 tablespoons sugar

1 apple, cored, diced
1 grapefruit, peeled, sectioned
1/2 cup celery, diced
lettuce leaves

Put chopped cranberries in bowl and sprinkle with sugar. Combine apple, grapefruit, and celery. Add cranberries and Orange-Honey Fruit Dressing. Mix and chill. Line salad bowl with lettuce leaves and fill bowl with fruit salad.

   Makes 6 servings.

# Orange-Honey
# Fruit Dressing

1 1/2 cups creamed cottage
   cheese
1/2 cup orange juice

1/2 cup honey
1/2 teaspoon ginger

Place cottage cheese in deep mixing bowl. Beat at medium speed. Slowly add orange juice, honey, and ginger. Beat dressing until smooth. Chill before serving.

   Makes 2 1/2 cups. (Serve on fruit salad.)

# Molasses-Citrus Salad

1 1/2 cups Molasses Dressing
  (see following recipe)
4 oranges, peeled, sliced
  crosswise
1 large Bermuda onion, sliced,
  separated into rings

2 beets, cooked, sliced
1 large avocado, peeled, seeded,
  sliced
2 grapefruits, peeled, sectioned
lettuce leaves

Line 4 chilled salad plates with lettuce. Arrange oranges, onion rings, beets, avocado, and grapefruit atop lettuce. Pour Molasses Dressing over each salad. Serve immediately.

  Makes 4 servings.

# Molasses Dressing

2/3 cup salad oil
1/2 cup lime juice
2 tablespoons molasses

1 teaspoon white pepper
1 teaspoon salt
1 teaspoon dry mustard

Combine all ingredients in screw-top jar. Cover and shake thoroughly.

  Makes about 1 1/2 cups. (Serve on citrus salad or avocado salad.)

Salads

# Pineapple Salad with Crab

1 cup Pineapple Salad Dressing
   (see following recipe)
1 pound cooked lump crabmeat,
   picked over
1 cup cooked rice, cooled
2 apples, cored, diced

8-ounce can chunky pineapple,
   drained
3 tablespoons snipped dill
sprigs of dill
lettuce leaves

Combine crabmeat, rice, pineapple, apples, and snipped dill in large mixing bowl. Add 1 cup Pineapple Dressing. Toss mixture. Cover and chill for about 1 hour.

Line deep salad bowl with lettuce leaves. Transfer crab mixture to salad bowl; garnish with sprigs of dill. Additional dressing may be served in side dish.

Makes 4 servings.

# Pineapple Salad Dressing

1/2 cup mayonnaise
2 tablespoons lemon juice

1/2 cup flaked coconut
1 cup pineapple yogurt

Combine mayonnaise and lemon juice. Add coconut to mayonnaise mixture. Fold in yogurt. Chill before serving.

Makes 2 cups. (Serve on fruit salad and molded salad.)

**ANNIE'S TIPS**

*Ripen fruit in bowl or basket at room temperature.*

# Yam Fruit Salad

2 cups Pineapple Salad Dressing
(see previous recipe)
5 yams, cooked, peeled, sliced

4 bananas, sliced
3 apples, cored and diced
1 cup golden raisins

Bake yams until tender but firm. Test in about 45 minutes. Peel yams while still warm. Combine diced yams, bananas, apples, and raisins. Toss salad with Pineapple Salad Dressing.
Makes 6 to 8 servings.

# Strawberry Delight

2 1/2 cups Strawberry Dressing
(see following recipe)
mint leaves
1 large honeydew, halved,
seeded, fiber removed

1 pint strawberries, hulled,
halved if large
1 cup seedless grapes

Peel melon and cut into wedges. Arrange melon wedges on 6 salad plates. Spoon Strawberry Dressing over melon wedges. Place strawberries and grapes on each plate atop dressing. Garnish with mint leaves.
Makes 6 servings.

# Strawberry Dressing

1 1/2 cups sour cream
1 tablespoon strawberry gelatin

1 teaspoon lemon juice
1 cup strawberries, chopped

Combine sour cream, gelatin, and lemon juice. Stir strawberries into sour cream mixture. Chill before serving.
Makes 2 1/2 cups. (Serve with fruit salad.)

Salads

# Cream Cheese Fruit Salad

3/4 cup Cream Cheese
   Dressing (see following recipe)
1 1/2 cups red grapes, split and
   seeded
1 large red apple, cored
   and diced

11/2 cups mandarin oranges,
   drained
1/4 cup slivered almonds
lettuce leaves

Combine grapes, diced apples, oranges, and almonds. Toss mixture with Cream Cheese Dressing. Serve on lettuce-lined salad plates.
   Makes 4 servings.

# Cream Cheese Dressing

3-ounce package cream
   cheese, softened
1 tablespoon honey

1/4 teaspoon salt
2 teaspoons lemon juice
1/4 cup orange juice

Combine cream cheese with honey and salt. Add lemon juice and orange juice and beat with electric mixer until smooth. Chill before serving.
   Makes 3/4 cup. (Serve on fruit salad.)

# Stuffed Peach Salad

3/4 cup Cream Cheese Dressing
   (see previous recipe)
8 canned peach halves, drained
1 cup coconut
1/2 cup celery, minced

1 cup pecans, chopped
1/2 teaspoon salt
pulp from peach halves
lettuce leaves

Remove small amount of pulp from cavity of each peach. Combine pulp with coconut, celery, pecans, and salt. Chill. Arrange 2 peach halves on 4 lettuce-lined individual salad plates. Fill cavity with chilled mixture. Garnish with Cream Cheese Dressing.
   Makes 4 servings.

ANNIE'S TIPS

*Refrigerate ripened fruit that you are not using to retard spoilage.*

# Stuffed Pear Salad

**3/4 cup Cream Cheese Dressing**
**(p.138)**
**2/3 cup fresh dates, pitted,**
**sliced**

*romaine leaves*
*8 canned pear halves, drained,*
*sliced*
*1 teaspoon slivered almonds*

Substitute orange juice with 1 teaspoon orange peel when preparing Cream Cheese Dressing. Add dates to dressing. Chill.

Line 4 salad plates with romaine. Arrange two pear halves on each salad plate. Spoon cream cheese mixture into the center of each pear. Garnish with slivered almonds.

Makes 4 servings.

ANNIE'S TIPS

*After cutting fruit, brush*
*lightly with lemon juice to*
*preserve color.*

# Salads Made with Potatoes, Rice, and Pasta

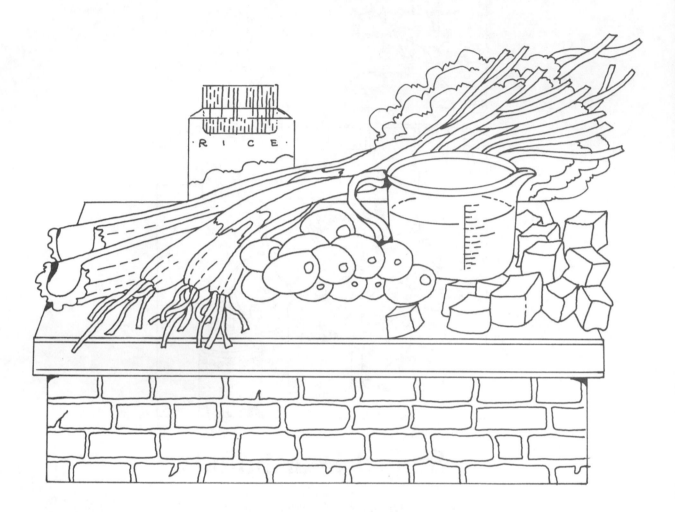

# Bologna Salad

2 cups Pickled Beet Sour Cream
   Dressing (see following recipe)
3 cups cooked potatoes, cubed
12 ounces chunk bologna, cubed
1 medium apple, cored and cubed
snipped parsley

1/2 cup pickled beets,
   cut in strips
1/4 cup dill pickle, chopped
1/4 cup onion, chopped
lettuce leaves

In mixing bowl, combine potatoes, bologna, apple, pickled beets, pickle, and onion. Toss gently to combine. Add Pickled Beet Sour Cream Dressing to bologna mixture. Chill for several hours before serving. Serve in lettuce-lined bowl, garnish with snipped parsley.

Makes about 6 servings.

# Pickled Beet
# Sour Cream Dressing

*1 cup sour cream*
*2 tablespoons pickled beet juice*
*1 tablespoon prepared mustard*
*1/2 teaspoon salt*

*1 cup pickled beets, drained*
*1/4 cup parsley clusters*
*1/4 teaspoon ground allspice*

Put all ingredients in blender. Blend until smooth. Chill before serving.

Makes about 2 cups. (Serve with a vegetable salad.)

ANNIE'S TIPS

*Storage: Washing before storage will promote decay.*

Salads

141

# Apple Raisin
# Potato Salad

*1 cup Quick Potato Salad Dressing
   (see following recipe)*
*3 hard cooking apples,
   peeled and cored*

*2 pounds new potatoes, boiled*
*1/4 cup dry white wine*
*1/2 cup white raisins*

Slice apples into 1/4-inch wedges; set aside. Cook potatoes, with skin on, in boiling salted water. Cook until tender, about 15 to 20 minutes. Drain, peel, and slice potatoes into 1/4-inch pieces while still warm. Put potatoes in deep serving dish and toss with wine.

Add apples and raisins to potatoes. Add Quick Potato Salad Dressing and toss mixture. Serve salad warm.

Makes 6 servings.

# Quick Potato
# Salad Dressing

*1/4 cup heavy cream*
*3 tablespoons white wine vinegar*
*2 tablespoons horseradish*
*2 teaspoons onion, grated*

*1 teaspoon salt*
*1/8 teaspoon white pepper*
*1/2 cup olive oil*

Combine all ingredients except olive oil in screw-top jar. Cover and shake thoroughly. Add olive oil and again cover and shake.

Makes about 1 cup. (Serve over warm potato salad.)

# Chicken and Brown Rice Toss

3/4 cup Herbed Sour Cream
    Dressing (p.114)
3 cups cooked brown rice
2 cups cooked chicken, cubed
1/2 cup celery, sliced

1/4 cup pitted ripe olives, sliced
2 tablespoons green onion, diced
1/2 cup cashew nuts,
    chopped coarsely
lettuce leaves

Combine cooked rice, chicken, celery, olives, and onion in large mixing bowl. Add Herbed Sour Cream Dressing. Toss mixture gently to coat. Cover bowl and chill for several hours. Before serving, add cashews and toss again. Turn mixture into lettuce-lined salad bowl.

    Makes 4 to 5 servings.

**ANNIE'S TIPS**

*Cook potatoes until just
tender. Never overcook.*

# Chicken-Potato Salad

1 1/2 cups Creamy Salad
   Dressing (p.109)
4 cups cooked potatoes, cubed
1/2 cup cooked chicken, cubed
8 ounces Swiss cheese,
   cut in strips

1/2 cup diced celery
1/2 cup green onion, sliced
1/2 cup radish, sliced
1/4 cup green pepper, chopped
3 hard-boiled eggs, diced
1/2 teaspoon salt

Gently toss all ingredients in large bowl; cover. Chill for several hours.

   Makes 6 servings.

# French-Style Bean
# and Potato Salad

1 cup French-Style Blue Cheese
   Dressing (p.119)
1 small head iceberg lettuce
6 medium red potatoes,
   cooked, peeled
1/2 pound French-style
   green beans

4 medium tomatoes, quartered
7-ounce can tuna,
   drained, flaked
12 pitted black olives
2 tablespoons capers

Cook potatoes in boiling salted water for 15 to 20 minutes. Drain, peel, and dice potatoes while still warm. Steam French-style green beans until just tender.

   Combine prepared potatoes and beans in large mixing bowl. Pour 1/2 cup French-Style Blue Cheese Dressing over mixture and toss gently. Cover and chill for several hours.

   Arrange lettuce leaves on large shallow serving plate. Add tomatoes to bean and potato mixture. Spoon vegetable mixture onto lettuce leaves. Add tuna, olives, and capers to salad plate. Pour 1/2 cup French-Style Blue Cheese Dressing over top of salad and serve at once.

   Makes 4 to 6 servings.

# French-Fry Potato Salad

3/4 cup Creamy Bacon
   Dressing (p.102)
16-ounce package frozen
   French-fried potatoes
1 1/2 teaspoons salt

4 hard-boiled eggs, chopped
1/2 cup radishes, sliced
1/2 cup celery, diced
2 tablespoons parsley
lettuce leaves

In a large pot, bring 4 cups of water to full boil. Carefully drop frozen fries into boiling water. Remove pot from heat immediately. Cover pot and let stand for 4 to 5 minutes. Drain potatoes into colander and spread potatoes onto paper towels. Sprinkle with salt.

In a large bowl, combine eggs, radishes, and celery. Add cooled potatoes. Add Creamy Bacon Dressing and toss mixture gently. Cover bowl and chill for several hours. Serve salad in lettuce-lined bowl and garnish with parsley.

Makes 8 servings.

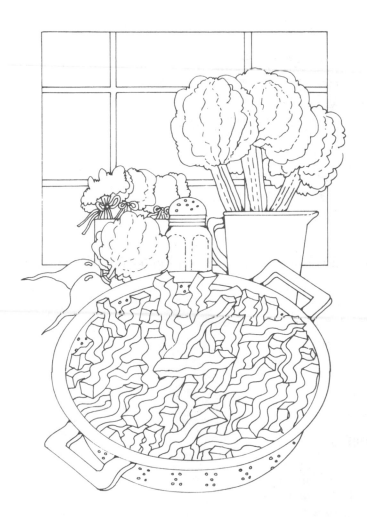

**Salads**

# Garden Macaroni Salad

1 cup Herbed Sour Cream
   Dressing (p.114)
4 cups cooked elbow macaroni,
   drained
1 cup cucumber, seeded and diced
1 cup celery, sliced

1/4 cup green pepper, diced
1/4 cup radishes, sliced thin
2 tablespoons scallions, sliced
2 tomatoes, seeded and diced
lettuce leaves

Gently toss together all ingredients. Cover and chill for several hours before serving. Serving in lettuce-lined salad bowl.
   Makes about 6 servings.

### ANNIE'S TIPS

*After cooking pasta, pour 1 cup cold water into pot; drain in colander and rinse quickly to wash off excess starch.*

# Macaroni and Cheese Salad

1 cup Special Yogurt Dressing
  (see following recipe)
4 cups cooked elbow macaroni,
  drained

2 cups leftover ham, cubed
1/2 cup aged Swiss cheese, cubed
1/2 cup mung bean sprouts
lettuce leaves

Gently toss all ingredients together. Cover and chill for several hours before serving. Serve in lettuce-lined salad bowl.
  Makes about 6 servings.

# Special Yogurt Dressing

1/2 cup yogurt
1 cup mayonnaise
1/4 small onion, minced

1 teaspoon Worcestershire sauce
1/8 teaspoon garlic powder
4 ounces Roquefort or blue
  cheese, crumbled

Mix all ingredients with electric mixer. Chill before serving.
  Makes 2 cups. (Serve with any vegetable salad.)

# Vegetable Rice Salad

1 cup Special Yogurt Dressing
  (see previous recipe)
6-ounce package long-grain
  and wild rice
1 cup diced celery

1 cup cubed tomato
1/2 cup diced cucumber
2 tablespoons chopped parsley
1/2 cup chopped soy nuts
lettuce leaves

Cook rice as directed on package; omit butter or margarine.
  Toss all ingredients together, except soy nuts. Cover bowl and chill for several hours. Line salad bowl with lettuce. Fill bowl with rice mixture. Garnish with soy nuts.
  Makes 6 servings.

Salads

# Macaroni and Cheese Salad Ring

2 1/4 cups Ginger Cheese
   Dressing (see following recipe)
4 cups cooked elbow macaroni,
   drained
1/4 cup diced pimento

2 tablespoons chopped onion
2 tablespoons chopped parsley
3/4 teaspoon salt
lettuce leaves
additional pimento and parsley

Combine macaroni and dressing in large bowl. Stir in pimento, onion, parsley, and salt. Cover bowl or press mixture into 9-inch ring mold. Chill several hours. Loosen sides with knife. Turn out on lettuce-lined serving plate. Garnish with additional pimento and parsley.

Makes 6 servings.

# Ginger Cheese Dressing

2 tablespoons milk
12-ounce carton creamed
   cottage cheese
1/2 cup mayonnaise

1/4 teaspoon salt
1/2 teaspoon ginger
2 tablespoons sugar

Blend all ingredients until smooth in blender or electric mixer. Chill well before serving.

Makes about 2 1/4 cups. (Serve with mixed salad greens or vegetables.)

ANNIE'S TIPS

*Pasta should be cooked al dente (8-to-10 minutes).*

# Macaroni Slaw

1 cup Yogurt Slaw Dressing
   (see following recipe)
4 cups cooked elbow macaroni,
   drained
3 cups finely shredded
   green cabbage

1 cup coarsely shredded carrot
1/2 cup finely chopped
   green pepper
3 tablespoons minced onion

Gently toss all ingredients except dressing. Add Yogurt Slaw Dressing to tossed ingredients. Stir gently until coated. Cover container and chill for several hours.
   Makes 7 servings.

# Yogurt Slaw Dressing

2 eggs, beaten
3 tablespoons honey
1 teaspoon salt

1 cup yogurt
1/4 cup lemon juice
1 teaspoon celery seed

In the top of a double boiler, blend all ingredients into smooth paste. Cook until smooth and thick.
   Makes about 2 cups. (Serve with a vegetable salad.)

ANNIE'S TIPS

*To refresh, plunge hot food into cold water to quickly stop the cooking process and avoid over-cooking.*

Salads

149

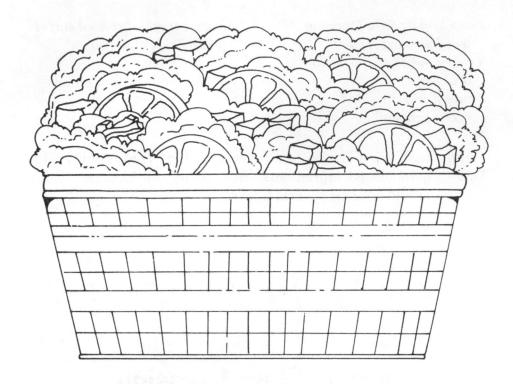

# Pepper Steak Salad

1 cup Caper Dressing
  (see following recipe)
1 cup cooked long-grain or
  brown rice
2 cups cooked beef,
  sliced thin and cut in strips

3 cups torn mixed salad greens
one 15 1/4-ounce can pineapple
  chunks, packed in natural juice
3 medium tomatoes, cut in wedges
1 green pepper, cut in strips
1/2 cup mung bean sprouts

Place beef in bowl. Pour Caper Dressing over beef. Cover and marinate for several hours in refrigerator. Place cooked rice in small mixing bowl; set aside.

To serve, place salad greens in large salad bowl. Drain marinade from beef into small mixing bowl with rice. Stir rice mixture. Put rice atop salad greens in a mound. Top with beef, pineapple chunks, tomato, green pepper, and sprouts. Salad is ready to be served or may be tossed lightly.

Makes 4 servings.

# Caper Dressing

1/4 cup capers, drained
1/3 cup salad oil
1/4 cup tarragon vinegar
2 tablespoons dry white wine

1 teaspoon sugar
1/2 teaspoon salt
1/2 teaspoon dry mustard
freshly ground pepper

If capers are large, cut in half. In screw-top jar combine all ingredients. Cover and shake.

Makes 1 cup. (Serve with salad greens or vegetable salad.)

**Salads**

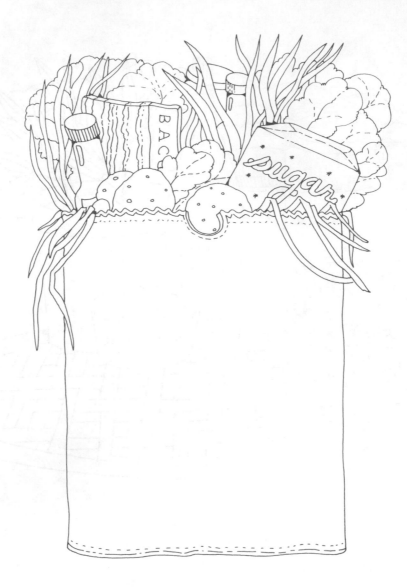

# Sweetcorn Salad

1/2 cup White Wine Dressing
  (p. 117)

2-3 drops Tabasco® sauce

1/2 teaspoon dry mustard

1 bay leaf

1 pound canned sweetcorn,
  drained

1 small green pepper,
  seeded, finely chopped

4 canned pimentos,
  drained, finely chopped

1 small onion, finely chopped

Combine Tabasco® sauce, dry mustard, bay leaf, and White Wine Dressing in mixing bowl. Combine sweetcorn, green pepper, pimentos, and onion in salad bowl.

Pour dressing mixture over sweetcorn mixture. Cover salad bowl and set aside at room temperature for at least 2 hours. Remove and discard bay leaf before serving.

Makes 4 to 6 servings.

# Tuna-Fruit
# Sea Shell Salad

*1 cup Yogurt Dressing Supreme*
  *(p.115)*
*4 cups cooked sea-shell*
  *macaroni, drained*
*one 7-ounce can tuna,*
  *drained and flaked*

*1 medium orange,*
  *peeled, seeded, and sectioned*
*1 medium apple,*
  *cored and sliced thin*
*1/3 cup dark seedless raisins*
*lettuce leaves*

Gently toss together all ingredients. Cover and chill for several hours before serving. Serve in lettuce-lined salad bowl.

Makes about 6 servings.

**Salads**

# Turkey and Garbanzo Bean Toss

1 cup Peppered Avocado Dressing
   (see following recipe)
15-ounce can garbanzo beans
2 cups cooked turkey, diced
1 cup celery, sliced
1/2 cup chopped green pepper
1/4 cup chopped green onion

1 medium tomato,
   seeded and diced
lettuce leaves
2 ounces Monterey Jack cheese,
   cut in strips
2 tablespoons snipped parsley

Rinse beans in cold water; drain. In large mixing bowl, combine beans, turkey, celery, green pepper, onion, and tomato. Fold Peppered Avocado Dressing into bean mixture. Cover bowl and chill for several hours.

To serve, pour mixture into lettuce-lined salad bowl. Top with cheese and parsley.

Makes 4 servings.

# Peppered Avocado Dressing

1 cup mayonnaise

1 ripe avocado, peeled, seeded, cubed

1/3 cup lemon juice

2 tablespoons milk

1 tablespoon honey

1 teaspoon salt

1/4 teaspoon hot pepper sauce

1/2 clove garlic

Place all ingredients in blender. Blend until garlic clove is liquefied. Chill before serving.

Makes 2 cups. (Serve with tossed salad greens.)

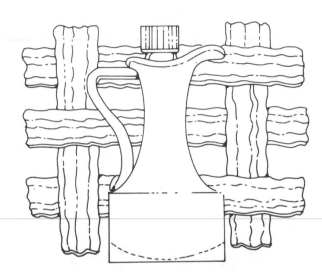

# Hot Potato Salad

3 pounds red potatoes, boiled

3/4 cup minced onion

1/4 cup minced celery

1/2 cup white wine vinegar

1 tablespoon sugar

salt

pepper

6 strips bacon, crumbled

3/4 teaspoon celery seed

1/4 cup minced parsley

Cook potato, with skin on, in boiling salted water in covered pot. Cook until tender, about 25 minutes. Drain, peel, and slice potatoes while still warm and set aside.

Sauté onion and celery in small amount of cooking oil for 1 minute. Add broth and vinegar. Season with sugar, salt, and pepper to taste. Add onion and celery mixture to potatoes. Add crumbled bacon, celery seed, and parsley. Toss and serve immediately.

Makes 8 servings.

# Salads Made in Molds

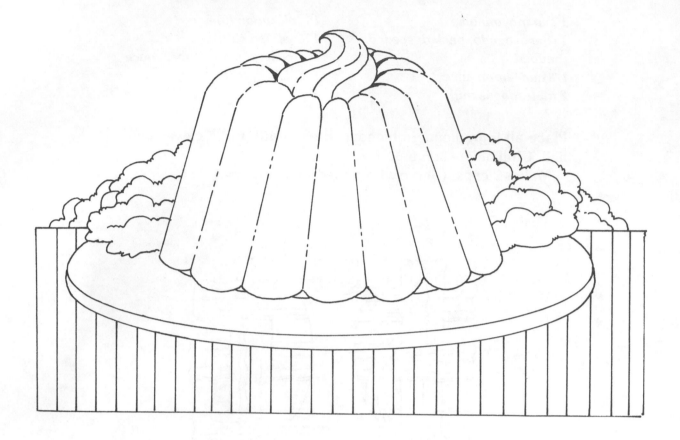

## Avocado Tuna
## Salad Ring

3 envelopes unflavored gelatin
1/4 cup lemon juice
3 avocados, peeled, seeded,
  and mashed
1 cup sour cream
1 cup mayonnaise
1/2 small onion, grated

1 tablespoon Worcestershire sauce
1 teaspoon celery salt
1/8 teaspoon pepper
lettuce leaves
tuna salad
5-cup ring mold

Dissolve unflavored gelatin in 1 cup boiling water. In mixing bowl, combine lemon juice, avocado, sour cream, mayonnaise, onion, Worcestershire, celery salt, and pepper. Blend mixture with electric mixer. Add gelatin to avocado mixture. Blend again. Pour gelatin and avocado mixture into mold. Chill until firm, about 3 to 4 hours.

Unmold onto lettuce-lined serving plate. Fill center of mold with tuna salad.

Makes 8 servings.

# Beet Cucumber Salad Ring

1 cup Cool Cucumber Sauce
   (see following recipe)
16-ounce can shoestring beets
1 envelope unflavored gelatin
1/4 cup sugar

dash salt
3 tablespoons lemon juice
1/2 small cucumber, sliced thin
lettuce leaves
3 1/2- or 4-cup ring mold

Drain beets, reserving liquid; set aside. Combine gelatin, sugar, and salt in small saucepan. Add enough water to beet liquid to make 1 3/4 cups. Add liquid to gelatin mixture. Cook and stir over low heat until gelatin dissolves. Stir in lemon juice.

Pour about 3/4 cup of gelatin mixture into ring mold. Arrange cucumbers in bottom of mold. Chill both gelatin mixtures until larger amount is partially set. Stir beets into larger amount of gelatin. Spoon over cucumbers in mold. Chill until firm. Unmold onto lettuce-lined serving plates. Serve with Cool Cucumber Sauce.

Makes 6 servings.

## ANNIE'S TIPS

*Use paper towel and small amount of mayonnaise to coat mold. For best results, always use size and shape of mold suggested in recipe.*

Salads

# Cool Cucumber Sauce

1/2 cup mayonnaise
1/2 cup lemon yogurt
1/2 cup cucumber, chopped
1 tablespoon chives, chopped

1 teaspoon chopped parsley
1/4 teaspoon salt
1/4 teaspoon dill weed

Combine all ingredients. Mix well. Chill before serving.
Makes 1 1/2 cups. (Serve with fresh vegetable salad or molded salad.)

# Cran-Apple
# Turkey Salad Mold

6-ounce package straw-
  berry-flavored gelatin
16-ounce can whole
  cranberry sauce
1 cup applesauce
1/2 cup port wine

1/4 cup walnuts, chopped
1/4 cup apple, peeled, chopped
lettuce leaves
sliced turkey
6 1/2-cup mold

Dissolve gelatin in 2 cups boiling water. Stir cranberry sauce, applesauce, and wine into gelatin. Chill until partially set. Fold walnuts and apples into gelatin. Pour mixture into mold and chill until firm, about 6 hours or overnight. Unmold onto lettuce-lined platter. Arrange turkey around mold.
Makes 10 to 12 servings.

# Cider Salad Mold

Fresh Fruit Dressing (p.133)
4 cups apple cider
4 whole cloves
4 inches stick cinnamon
two 3-ounce packages lemon-
  flavored gelatin

1 orange, peeled, seeded,
  sectioned
1 unpared apple, cored, diced
lettuce leaves
5 1/2-cup ring mold

In saucepan, combine cider, cloves, and cinnamon. Cover saucepan and simmer for 15 minutes; strain. Dissolve gelatin in hot cider. Pour 1 cup of cider mixture into mold. Chill until partially set. Keep remaining gelatin at room temperature.
Arrange orange sections over gelatin in mold. Chill again until almost firm. Also chill remaining gelatin until partially set. Fold

apples into partially-set gelatin. Carefully spoon mixture into mold. Chill until firm.

Unmold onto lettuce-lined plate. Fill center of cider salad mold with Fresh Fruit Dressing.

Makes 8 servings.

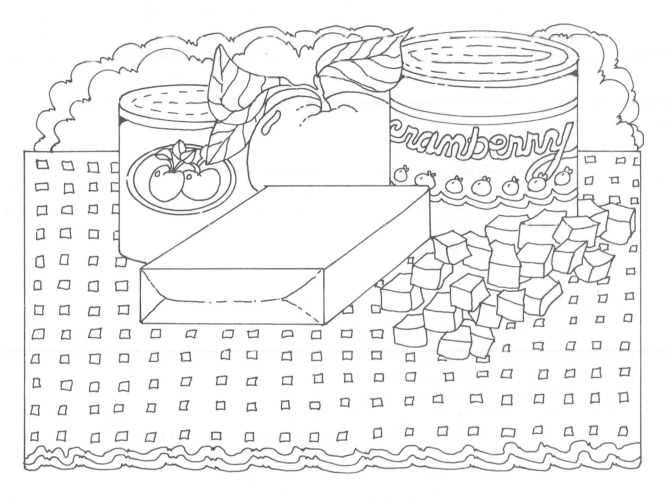

# Cottage Cheese Peach Salad

*3-ounce package peach-*
  *flavored gelatin*
*1/2 cup canned peach slices,*
  *drained and diced*
*lettuce leaves*

*1 cup creamed cottage cheese*
*4 tablespoons sour cream*
*slivered almonds*
  *or chopped chives*
*4 individual-sized molds*

Dissolve gelatin in 1 cup boiling water. Add 3/4 cup cold water or reserved juice from peaches. Chill until partially set. Fold peaches into gelatin. Spoon gelatin mixture into molds. Chill until firm.

Salads

Line 4 individual dessert dishes with lettuce. Place 1/4 cup cottage cheese into each dish. Unmold gelatins atop cottage cheese. Garnish each mold with 1 tablespoon sour cream. Top with almonds or chives.

Makes 4 servings.

# Cucumber and Grape Salad

two 3-ounce packages lemon-
 flavored gelatin
3 tablespoons orange juice
6 tablespoons lemon juice
1 tablespoon onion,
 very finely chopped
1/8 teaspoon cayenne pepper

1/2 teaspoon salt
1 large cucumber,
 peeled, thinly sliced
1 pound seedless white grapes,
 halved
lettuce leaves
6-cup mold

Dissolve gelatin in 2 1/2 cups boiling water. Stir in orange juice and lemon juice. Add onion, cayenne, and salt. Chill until mixture is partially set.

Reserve 10 cucumber slices and 10 grapes. Set aside. Fold remaining cucumber and grapes into gelatin mixture. Spoon mixture into mold. Chill until firm.

Arrange lettuce leaves on serving plate. Unmold gelatin onto lettuce leaves. Garnish salad with reserved cucumber slices and grapes.

Makes 8 servings.

# Frozen Fruitcake Salad

1 cup sour cream
4 tablespoons cherry yogurt
2 tablespoons lemon juice
1/2 cup sugar
1 teaspoon vanilla
13-ounce can crushed
   pineapple, drained
lettuce leaves

2 medium bananas, diced
1/2 cup red candied cherries,
   halved
1/2 cup green candied cherries,
   halved
1/2 cup walnuts, chopped
4 1/2-cup ring mold

In mixing bowl, blend together sour cream, yogurt, sugar, lemon juice, and vanilla. Fold in fruit and nuts. Pour into ring mold. Freeze for several hours or overnight. Unmold onto lettuce-lined plate. Let stand for 10 minutes before serving.

   Makes 8 servings.

# Fruit Squares

two 3-ounce packages lime-
   flavored gelatin
1 teaspoon lemon juice
8-ounce package cream
   cheese, softened

1 cup diced fresh fruit
   (strawberries, peaches, grapes)
lettuce leaves
8-inch square pan

Dissolve gelatin in 2 cups boiling water. Reserve 1/2 cup of gelatin, add 1/2 cup cold water, and set aside. Add 3/4 cup water and lemon juice to remaining gelatin. Very slowly blend gelatin into softened cream cheese. Chill until partially set.

   Fold fruit into chilled gelatin. Spoon gelatin mixture into pan. Chill again for about 15 minutes. Top with reserved clear gelatin and chill until firm, about 3 hours. To serve, cut into squares and place on lettuce-lined individual salad plates.

   Makes 8 servings.

Salads

# Grapefruit Ring

two 3-ounce packages lemon-
  flavored gelatin
1/3 cup frozen lemonade
  concentrate
1 cup red grapes,
  halved and seeded
chopped celery tops

2 grapefruits, peeled, seeded,
  and sectioned
1/2 cup celery, chopped
creamed cottage cheese,
  enough to fill center of mold
6-cup ring mold

Dissolve gelatin in 1 1/2 cups boiling water. Stir in lemonade concentrate and 2 cups cold water. Chill until mixture is partially set. Fold grapefruit sections, grapes, and celery into mixture. Spoon gelatin mixture into mold.

Chill until firm. Unmold. Fill center of mold with cottage cheese and garnish with chopped celery tops.

Makes 8 servings.

# Lime-Walnut Salad

3-ounce package lime-
  flavored gelatin
1 cup crushed pineapple
  with syrup
2 stalks celery, chopped

12-ounce carton creamed
  cottage cheese
1/2 cup walnuts, chopped fine
5-cup mold

Dissolve gelatin in 1 cup boiling water. Add pineapple with syrup to gelatin. Chill until partially set. Beat cottage cheese with electric mixer for 1 minute. Add gelatin to cottage cheese. Mix until well blended. Add celery and walnuts to gelatin mixture. Pour into mold. Chill until firm.

Makes 6 servings.

ANNIE'S TIPS

*Substitute water with fruit juice whenever reserved juice is available.*

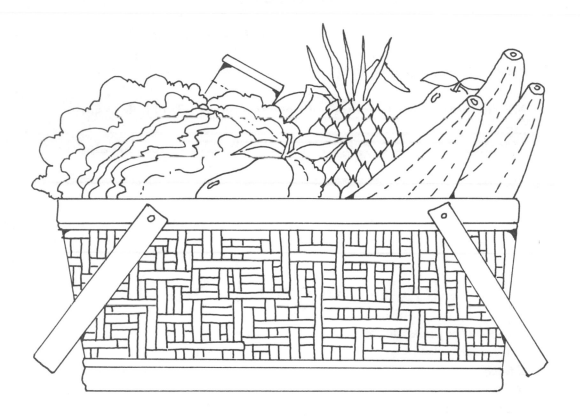

# Molded Waldorf Salad

1 2/3 cups Zesty Blue Cheese
   Dressing (see following recipe)
3-ounce package lime-
   flavored-gelatin
1/2 cup sauterne
2 tablespoons lemon juice

1/2 cup celery, chopped
1/4 cup walnuts
1 red apple, cored, diced
lettuce leaves
3-cup mold

Dissolve lime-flavored gelatin in 1 1/4 cups boiling water. Add sauterne and lemon juice. Chill until partially set. Add celery, walnuts, and apple. Pour into mold and chill until firm. Unmold onto lettuce leaves, and serve with a side dish of Zesty Blue Cheese Dressing.

   Makes 4 to 6 servings.

Salads

# Zesty Blue Cheese Dressing

1 cup mayonnaise
4 ounces blue cheese, crumbled
1/4 cup dry white wine

1 tablespoon grated onion
4–5 drops hot pepper sauce

Mix all ingredients together with electric mixer. Chill before serving.

    Makes about 1 2/3 cups. (Serve with vegetable or tossed salad.)

# Molded Vegetable Salad

two 3-ounce packages lemon-
   flavored gelatin
2 teaspoons salt
3 tablespoons lemon juice
1/2 cup cucumber,
   seeded and diced

1/2 cup cooked peas
1/2 cup cooked carrots
2 tablespoons pimento, chopped
lettuce leaves
5-cup mold

Dissolve gelatin and salt in 2 cups boiling water. Pour lemon juice into measuring cup. Add enough water to equal 1 1/2 cups. Add to gelatin. Chill mixture until partially set. Fold cucumber, peas, carrots, and pimento into gelatin. Pour mixture into mold. Chill until firm, about 4 hours. Unmold onto lettuce-lined serving plate.

    Makes 8 servings.

# Sweet Yogurt Dressing

1/2 cup yogurt
4 tablespoons honey

2 tablespoons lemon juice
1/8 teaspoon cinnamon

Mix all ingredients together by hand. Chill well before serving.

    Makes about 1/4 cup. (Serve with mixed salad greens or vegetable salad.)

# Pear Cucumber Mold

3-ounce package lime-
  flavored gelatin

2 tablespoons lemon juice

2 cups canned pears, drained,
  chopped

3/4 cup cucumbers,
  chopped fine

1 cup cream-style cottage
  cheese

lettuce leaves

1 cucumber, sliced thin

2 tablespoons minced chives

4-cup ring mold

Dissolve gelatin in 1 cup boiling water. Add lemon juice and 1 cup cold water. Chill until partially set.

Add pears and cucumbers to gelatin. Pour mixture into mold and chill until firm, about 3 hours. Unmold onto lettuce-lined salad plate. Fill center of mold with cottage cheese. Garnish cottage cheese with chives. Arrange sliced cucumbers around mold.

Makes 4 to 6 servings.

### ANNIE'S TIPS

*Partially set means the consistency of unbeaten egg whites.*

Salads

# Pear and Lime
# Salad Mold

16-ounce can Bartlett pears,
   drained and diced
1 package lime-flavored gelatin
2/3 cup reserved pear juice
1/4 cup lemon juice

1/4 teaspoon salt
1/4 cup pimento, diced
1 cup cabbage, finely shredded
lettuce leaves
6 individual-sized molds

Drain canned pears and reserve the juice. Dissolve gelatin in 1 cup boiling water. Add reserved pear juice, lemon juice, and salt to gelatin. Chill until partially set.

Add pears, pimento, and cabbage to gelatin. Pour into individual molds and chill until set. Unmold onto lettuce-lined salad plates.

Makes 6 servings.

# Red Top Egg Salad

3-ounce package lemon-
  flavored gelatin
1/4 cup lemon juice
1/2 cup mayonnaise
1/2 teaspoon salt
13 1/2-ounce can
  tomato aspic
6 hard-boiled eggs, chopped

1/2 cup celery, minced
1/2 cup carrot, grated
2 tablespoons snipped parsley
1/2 teaspoon onion,
  finely grated
lettuce leaves
1 hard-boiled egg, sliced
6-cup mold

Dissolve gelatin in 1 cup boiling water. Add 1/2 cup cold water and lemon juice to gelatin. Chill until partially set.

Melt aspic in saucepan over low heat. Add 1/4 cup water. Pour aspic into mold. Set mold aside; do not chill.

Fold chopped eggs, carrot, parsley, and onion into partially-set lemon gelatin. Carefully spoon gelatin and egg mixture atop the aspic; chill until firm, about 4 to 6 hours. Unmold onto lettuce-lined salad plate and garnish with sliced egg.

Makes 6 servings.

# Sangria Salad

2 envelopes unflavored gelatin
1/2 cup sugar
1 1/2 cups water
1 1/4 cups rosé wine
1 cup orange juice
2 tablespoons lemon juice

3 oranges, peeled, seeded,
  sectioned
1 large apple, cored,
  cut into chunks
1 cup red grapes, halved and
  seeded
6 1/2-cup mold

In saucepan, combine gelatin and sugar. Stir in 1 1/2 cups water. Cook and stir until gelatin dissolves. Remove saucepan from heat. Stir rosé wine, orange juice, and lemon juice into gelatin mixture. Chill until partially set.

Pour about 2 cups gelatin into mold and top with orange sections. Alternate remaining gelatin with apples and grapes. Chill until firm. Unmold. Garnish with additional grapes, if desired.

Makes 8 to 10 servings.

Salads

# Seafood Salad

1 envelope unflavored gelatin
3 tablespoons lemon juice
1/4 teaspoon salt
dash cayenne
3/4 cup mayonnaise
2 hard-boiled eggs, chopped
1 cup celery, chopped

1/2 cup tiny cooked shrimp
one 7-ounce can crabmeat,
    all cartilage removed
lettuce leaves
1 cup small cooked shrimp,
    peeled and cleaned
5-cup ring mold

Dissolve gelatin in 2/3 cup boiling water. Add lemon juice, salt, cayenne, and mayonnaise to gelatin. Chill until partially set. In bowl, combine eggs, celery, tiny shrimp, and crabmeat. Add gelatin mixture.

Pour into mold and chill until firm. Unmold onto lettuce leaves. Fill center of mold with cooked shrimp.

Makes 6 to 8 servings.

ANNIE'S TIPS

*Almost firm means gelatin feels sticky to the touch.*

# Spiced Peach Salad

29-ounce can peaches
4 medium oranges
2 teaspoons allspice
6-ounce package lemon-
   flavored gelatin

1/2 cup pecans, chopped
1/2 cup maraschino cherries
lettuce leaves
8-cup mold

Drain peaches and reserve syrup. Chop peaches. Peel and section the oranges over a bowl to catch the juice. Combine the juice with reserved syrup. If necessary add enough water to measure 2 cups. Set aside.

Dissolve gelatin in 2 cups boiling water. Add allspice to gelatin. Add the 2 cups of juice and syrup combination. Chill until partially set.

Add peaches, orange sections, pecans, and cherries to gelatin. Pour into mold and chill for about 6 hours or overnight. Unmold onto lettuce-lined serving plate.

Makes 10 to 12 servings.

Salads

# Strawberry Yogurt Mold

2 envelopes unflavored gelatin
1 cup lemonade
2 cups ginger ale
3/4 cup strawberry yogurt
1/4 teaspoon salt
6-cup mold

1 1/2 cups fresh strawberries,
  hulled and sliced
1/4 cup slivered blanched
  almonds
1 cup fresh whole strawberries,
  hulled

Heat lemonade in saucepan. Stir in gelatin until dissolved. Pour gelatin into large bowl. Add ginger ale, yogurt, and salt. Beat gelatin mixture with wire whisk until smooth. Chill mixture until partially set.

Fold strawberries and almonds into gelatin. Pour mixture into mold and chill until firm. Unmold onto lettuce-lined serving plate. Arrange whole strawberries around mold. Serve with a sauce dish of strawberry yogurt, if desired.

Makes 6 to 8 servings.

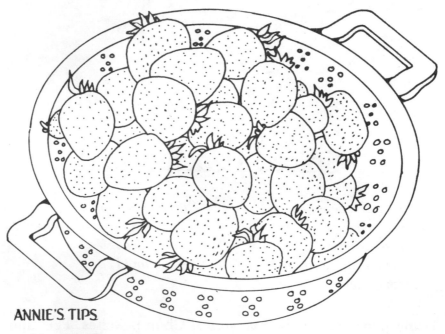

## ANNIE'S TIPS

To unmold, run knife carefully around edge of mold. Place serving plate upside-down on top of mold. Invert mold and plate together. A sharp tap on the top of mold is sometimes necessary after this procedure. If the mold sticks, rub it gently with a hot, damp towel, or turn the mold and plate over and repeat the entire process.

Salads

# Tomato Ring

*2 envelopes unflavored gelatin*
*1/2 cup hot chicken broth*
*1 small onion, grated*
*2 drops Tabasco® sauce*
*1 tablespoon Worcestershire*
*1/2 teaspoon celery salt*

*2 cups tomato juice*
*1 1/2 tablespoons lemon juice*
*1 cup mixed cooked vegetables*
*lettuce leaves*
*4-cup ring mold*

In a saucepan dissolve gelatin in hot chicken broth. Remove saucepan from heat. Add onion, Tabasco®, Worcestershire, and celery salt to gelatin. Stir mixture until well blended. Add tomato juice, lemon juice, and 1 cup cold water to gelatin mixture.

Pour into mold. Chill until firm, about 4 hours. Unmold onto lettuce-lined salad plate. Fill center of mold with mixed vegetables.

**Makes 6 servings.**

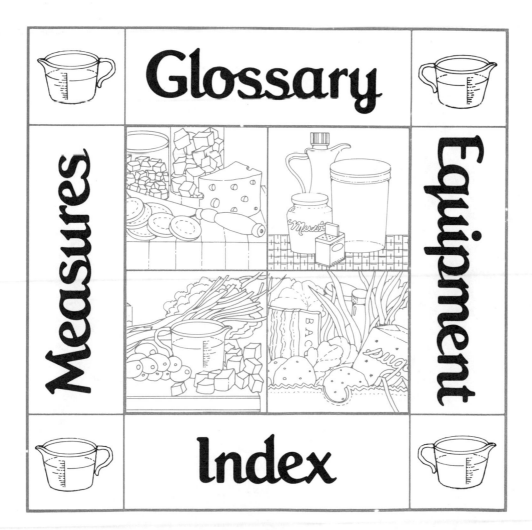

Glossary

Measures

Equipment

Index

# Weights and Measures

### Customary

3 teaspoons = 1 tablespoon

4 tablespoons = 1/4 cup

5 1/3 tablespoons = 1/3 cup

12 tablespoons = 3/4 cup

16 tablespoons = 1 cup

2 cups = 1 pint

2 pints = 1 quart

4 quarts = 1 gallon

1 pound = 16 ounces

1 fluid ounce = 2 tablespoons

16 fluid ounces = 1 pint

### Metric

1 liter = 1000 milliliters

1 liter = 10 deciliters

1 kilogram = 1000 grams

# Equivalents

### Customary

1/5 teaspoon = 1 milliliter

1 teaspoon = 5 milliliters

1 tablespoon = 15 milliliters

1/5 cup = 50 milliliters (approx.)

1 cup = 240 milliliters

1 pint = 470 milliliters

1 quart = .95 liter

1 gallon = 3.8 liters

1 fluid ounce = 30 milliliters

1 ounce dry weight = 28 grams

1 pound = 454 grams (approx. 1/2 kilogram)

### Metric

1 milliliter = .034 fluid ounce

1 liter = 1.06 quarts

1 liter = .264 gallon

1 gram = .035 ounce

1 kilogram = 2.205 pounds (35 ounces)

# Basic Kitchen Equipment

**Chopping** *or* **cutting board:** 1. made of durable hardwood about one inch thick. 2. acrylic, thought by many to be more sanitary.

**Electric blender:** for grinding, grating, puréeing, and blending food.

**Electric food processor:** accomplishes all the jobs of an electric blender and many others.

**Food mill:** for puréeing, mashing, and grinding almost any food; can be used instead of blender or food processor.

**Grater:** for grating and slicing; the best model stands upright and has several sizes of teeth and a slicer.

**Kettle:** a large heavy pot with a cover, about 8-10 quart capacity.

**Knives:** 1. chopping—a wide 8-inch blade for chopping, mincing, and dicing fruits, vegetables, and meat. 2. paring—a 3- to 3 1/2-inch blade for peeling and cutting small fruits and vegetables. 3. utility—a 5- to 7-inch blade for peeling and chopping large fruits and vegetables, and trimming meat.

**Measuring cups:** 1. glass for measuring liquids; 1-cup size and 1-quart size, with pouring lip. 2. metal for measuring solids; a graduated set of 1/4 cup, 1/3 cup, 1/2 cup, and 1 cup.

**Measuring spoons:** a standard set of 1/4 teaspoon, 1/2 teaspoon, 1 teaspoon, and 1 tablespoon; a second set comes in handy.

**Mixing bowls:** glass, pottery, or stainless steel; a graduated set of sizes.

**Saucepans:** 2-quart, 3- to 3 1/2-quart, and 5-quart; all with covers.

**Sieve:** an instrument with a meshed or perforated bottom, used for straining liquids.

**Tureen:** a deep, covered vessel from which cooked foods are served at the table.

**Whisk:** wire or wooden; an implement, usually loops held together in a handle, for beating and whipping; 8- to 10-inch size.

**Wooden spoons:** unvarnished wood for beating and stirring; 10- to 12-inch size.

# Glossary of Terms Used in This Book

**Beat:** to mix ingredients together with a circular up-and-down motion, using a whisk, a spoon, or a rotary electric beater.

**Bisque:** a thick cream soup, often made from fish or vegetable purées.

**Blend:** to stir, rather than beat, the ingredients until they are thoroughly combined.

**Boil:** to heat or cook in a liquid whose temperature reaches 212 degrees F; the surface will be broken by a steady bubbling action.

**Bouillabaisse:** a soup or stew containing several kinds of fish and shellfish; usually prepared with oil, tomatoes, and spices.

**Bouillon:** a clear seasoned broth made from poultry, meat, fish, or vegetables; also commercially prepared bouillon dissolved in boiling water.

**Bouillon cube:** a small cube of dehydrated beef, chicken, or vegetable stock.

**Bouillon cup:** a small vessel with two handles in which bouillon is served.

**Bouquet garni:** a small bundle of herbs wrapped and tied together in a piece of cheesecloth.

**Broth:** water that has been boiled with meat, fish, or vegetables and then strained.

**Brush on:** to apply a liquid to the surface of food with a small brush.

**Chill:** to make cold, not frozen, in the refrigerator.

**Chop:** to cut into small pieces.

**Chowder:** a soup or stew made of fish or vegetables which contains potatoes and onions, among other ingredients and seasonings.

**Clarify:** to make a substance pure or clear.

**Coat:** to cover food lightly but thoroughly with either a liquid or dry substance.

**Coconut milk:** a liquid obtained from fresh coconut meat.

**Coconut water:** the liquid within the fruit of the fresh coconut.

**Combine:** to mix or blend together two or more ingredients.

**Consommé:** a strong clear soup made by simmering meat and bones to extract their nutritive properties.

**Cool:** to allow to stand until heat has reduced.

**Core:** to remove the inedible central portion of certain fruits and vegetables.

**Crisp:** to make firm (leafy vegetables such as lettuce are washed, dried, and chilled).

**Crouton:** a small piece of fried or toasted bread used in soups as a garnish.

**Crush:** to mash fruits and vegetables, for example, until they lose their shape.

**Cube:** to cut into small, equal-sized squares, generally 1/4 to 1/2 inch.

**Dice:** to cut into very small, even cubes 1/4 to 1/2 inch long.

**Dissolve:** to make a solution by adding liquid to a solid substance or by heating a solid until it melts.

**Drain:** to remove liquid, usually by allowing food to stand in a strainer or colander until liquid has drained off.

**Fines herbes:** a mixture of minced herbs—parsley, chives, tarragon—used to flavor foods.

**Flake:** to break into small pieces with a fork, as with cooked fish.

**Fold:** to add or mix by gently turning one part over another with a spoon.

**Froth:** an aggregation of bubbles formed in or on an agitated liquid.

**Garnish:** to decorate or accompany a dish by adding other foodstuffs, such as snipped herbs.

**Grate:** to reduce a food to small particles by rubbing it on the teeth of a grater.

**Grind:** to reduce foods like herbs and spices to a fine, powdery consistency using a mortar and pestle.

**Gumbo:** a stew or thick soup containing okra.

**Hull:** to remove the calyx, or hull, of certain fruits such as the strawberry and raspberry.

**Julienne:** food, such as carrots or cheese, cut into thin, match-like strips.

**Madrilène:** a consommé flavored with tomato, frequently jelled and served cold.

**Marinade:** a liquid in which food is placed to enhance its flavor and to make it more tender.

**Marinate:** to let stand in a seasoned vinegar-oil mixture.

**Mash:** to soften and break down food by using the back of a spoon or by forcing through a ricer.

**Mince:** to cut or chop into very fine pieces.

**Mix:** to blend or stir together two or more ingredients.

**Pare:** to remove the outer covering and stem of a fruit or vegetable with a knife or other peeling tool.

**Partially set:** having the consistency of unbeaten egg whites.

**Peel:** 1. to remove the skin or rind of a fruit or vegetable with a knife or other peeling tool. 2. the skin or rind of a fruit or vegetable.

**Pith:** the white membrane under the rind of citrus fruits.

**Poach:** to cook food in a liquid that is barely simmering.

**Potage:** the French word for soup.

**Preheat:** to heat an oven or broiler to a desired temperature before using; usually takes about 10 minutes.

**Purée:** to force food through a sieve or food mill (or process in a blender or food processor) to obtain a thick, smooth liquid.

**Refresh:** to plunge hot food into cold water, quickly stopping the cooking process.

**Rind:** the outer skin of a fruit or vegetable.

**Sauté:** to cook briefly in a small amount of hot fat.

**Scramble:** to cook in a pan, mixing quickly.

**Set:** used in reference to liquids which have congealed and retained their shape.

**Shred:** to cut or break into thin pieces.

**Sieve:** 1. to put or force through a sieve. 2. a sieved or processed food.

**Simmer:** to cook a liquid barely at the boiling point; the surface should show only a few bubbles breaking slowly.

**Skim:** to remove a substance from the surface of a liquid.

**Steam:** to cook by means of vapor from a boiling liquid rising through the food.

**Stock:** a strained liquid in which meat, poultry, fish, bones, or vegetables and seasonings have been (or will be) cooked.

**Tender:** soft or delicate in substance; cooked to a delicate or soft texture.

**Unmold:** to remove from a mold.

**Whisk:** to whip with a whisk or other beating implement.

# Index

# Index

# Index

## Cold Soups

# Index

# Index

# NOTES & FAVORITE RECIPES

# NOTES & FAVORITE RECIPES

# NOTES & FAVORITE RECIPES

# NOTES & FAVORITE RECIPES